TALK YOURSELF OUT OF IT

DR. ROBERT A. RUSSELL

Audio Enlightenment Press

Giving Voice to the Wisdom of the Ages

Printed in the United States of America

First Printing, 2022
ISBN 978-1-941489-89-5

www.RobertARussell.Org

DEDICATED in loving gratitude to my mother, whose faith and life are a constant source of help and inspiration to me.

Table of Contents

INTRODUCTION

A GREAT DISCOVERY

One of the greatest discoveries in the field of psychic therapeutics and healing was made when Phineas Quimby discovered that by hypnotizing a patient he could not only diagnose the particular mental or physical ill from which the patient was suffering but could also talk him out of it. His second great discovery was that he had within himself the power and spiritual ability to diagnose the illness and heal the patient while he was in full possession of all his faculties. Furthermore, the patient always emerged from the experience in improved mental as well as physical health.

Quimby's treatment was simple but effective. Sitting quietly beside his patient and not allowing him to utter a word, Quimby would say something like this: "Now, as a matter of fact, you are a spiritual being; you are made out of God, out of pure Spirit. You are really perfect, but you are ignorant of your own perfection. You represent the man of ignorance, and I represent the man of wisdom. The man of ignorance goes around surrounded by his opinions, most of which are false. I can see all these opinions. I enter these opinions and explain that they are false. I see also that you do not need to die, for disease is externalization of thought. This stuff out of which you are made is fluid in its original state; and it can just as well be in perfect shape as in imperfect. You are surrounded by the opinions of the clergy, the doctors, and friends. You are afraid that you are going to die. It is all a mistake." Through this method Quimby healed hundreds, and his answer to the curious was always this: "My explanations is my cure."

Let us turn now to another and more recent discovery made by an eminent medical man in Europe — a discovery that is the basis of the theories presented in this book and in its companion volume *Talk Yourself Into It*. This doctor, discovering that a patient desired greatly to talk to him about herself, allowed her to recite her troubles to him. She talked for days; and as she talked, he discovered that she was gradually getting well. She was talking the disease out of herself. Putting two and two together, this man made up his mind that he had hit upon a great truth; at this moment, of the greatest discoveries ever made in the medical profession had its origin.

The doctor in question decided that this woman in talking to him had unburdened herself of the thing that was causing her sickness. From that discovery came the science that we call Analytical Psychology. This book is the metaphysical adaptation of that principle. If talks between two persons can produce such wonderful results, conversations between the conscious and subconscious minds (talking to one's self) can produce even greater results, for the entire action takes place within and upon the mind of the one giving the treatment.

If the soul is the medium between God and man, between heaven and earth, between the Absolute and the relative, and if all the inhibiting, disturbing, and tangled ideas that affect the body originate in the soul, we can unquestionably change the effect or action of the Law by changing the subjective causes (by talking them out of ourselves).

This is no hit-or-miss method; it is a definite technique for dislodging any belief in the subconscious mind that denies the greater blessings and for replacing it with the belief that accepts all Good as the rightful heritage of the child of God.

CHAPTER 1

TALKING TO YOURSELF

"What she said to herself was this. . ." MATT. 9:21. (Moffatt)

We all talk to ourselves at times, and what we say to ourselves is of the utmost importance. What we say to ourselves is what the world say back to us. Of course, we are affected by what others say to us, but we are influenced much more by what we say to ourselves. Tell me the kind of conversations you habitually hold with yourself, and I will tell you the kind of health, circumstances, and income you have. Tell me how you talk to yourself, and I will tell you what you are now and what you are likely to become.

"A word fitly spoken," says an ancient seer, "is like apples of gold in pictures of silver." Whether we talk to ourselves or to others, our words have the power to build or to destroy, to purify or to pollute, to heal or to kill, to help or to hinder, to enfeeble or to empower. There is no way to measure the endless harm accomplished by the wrong word nor the endless good accomplished by the right word. The Bible tells us that the power of life and death is in the tongue. There are words that have the power to change the whole course of our lives, to revolutionize our careers, to transform our bodies, and to life us into Heaven. There are other words that bind, cripple, weaken, paralyze, despoil, and damn. "By thy words," said Jesus, "thou shalt be justified, and by thy words thou shalt be condemned." When we realize that we put into the word what is to come out of it, we will speak only words that are wholesome and true.

But what do you say when you talk to yourself? Do you talk baby talk? Are you coddling, alibiing, pitying, doubting, dividing, isolating, or crippling yourself? Are you lessening your chances of recovery by continually telling yourself that you are sick? Are you talking double talk, saying one thing with your lips and another thing with your heart? Or are you telling the truth about yourself? Realize now that you have the power to talk yourself out of anything you wish, and start today to exercise the power and dominion of your word.

THE LAW OF EXPULSION

You talk yourself into the right things by building a mental equivalent for them, and you talk yourself out of the wrong things by devitalizing the mental equivalents that are holding them in place. You give substance, power, and form to the right mental equivalent by changing your thought, interest, and attention into it; and you destroy the wrong mental equivalent by changing your thought out of it (withdrawing the attention that gives it power) and by substituting a stronger and more perfect image in its place. You do not attack the wrong mental equivalent frontally with personal effort, thought, or will; you merely ignore the evil and center yourself in the good.

The Law of Mind says that you can change an evil effect only by changing its cause and that you can get rid of one mental equivalent only by substituting another. The process is very similar to changing the spark plugs in your car. If a spark plug is causing trouble and disturbing the rhythm and action of the car, you replace it with a good one to restore the perfect functioning of the motor. That is what happens in the subconscious mind when you substitute the right belief or mental equivalent for the wrong one. Harmony and perfection are restored, and life returns to normal. For every effect, there is a corresponding cause; to change the effect, we must first change the cause.

There are many ways to change a subjective cause, but the most effective way is by audibly talking yourself out of the troublesome thoughts and beliefs while keeping your thought changed into the new and more perfect image you are seeking to bring forth. It makes no difference how terrifying the appearances (effects) may be, the secret of success in expelling the things you do not want is to keep your thought (power) centered on the things you do want. By persistently thinking right, you build a new mental equivalent that will eventually appear in your life.

SUBJECTIVE FORMATION

"Until Christ be formed in you." GAL. 4:19.

The real purpose in talking to ourselves about the things we want from God is twofold: to disassociate certain beliefs in our minds, and to give proper direction to the subconscious self. In other words, we tell ourselves the truths we wish to embody , and then we send them down (through our realization) into the creative activity of the subconscious mind.

To the Person unaccustomed to this type of treatment, it may seem difficult; but as in every other worthwhile achievement in life, the more we practice, the easier the process becomes. Choose a suitable time and a place where you will not be disturbed; assume the position you use for the Silence or Meditation. Breathe deeply, normally, evenly, and relax from head to foot until your body no longer makes any demands upon your consciousness. Now discipline the human mind, pressing out of it all thoughts that have no bearing upon the ideal you are seeking to materialize. Hold your mind to the subject in hand as you would hold your car to the center of a dangerous and narrow road, remembering that the outer mind is capricious, rebellious, and undisciplined. It is likely an unruly child who can be made to behave only by much patience, training, firmness, and determination. No matter how the old habits and beliefs may seem to contradict this new mental equivalent, hold persistently to it until it penetrates the subconscious self and gains dominion in your consciousness.

The next two steps are comparatively easy. When you have brought the field of consciousness to the desired condition and centered your mind in God, state the truth which you wish to impress on the subconscious mind in as compact and convincing terms as possible. Then hold in it realization while talking to yourself about it until it forms in you a consciousness of itself. When the idea or statement begins to act upon your consciousness, a great peace (sense of fulfillment) will come over you, and you will know that the work has been done. You supply the word; God gives it form.

UNTHINKING

"I know that the way of man is not in himself; it is not in man that walketh to direct his step." JER. 10:23.

When we speak of talking ourselves out of certain undesirable and unwanted things, we really mean *un*speaking, *un*thinking, *un*learning, *un*knowing, and *un*feeling them. We spoke, thought, learned, and felt them into existence in the beginning by our wrong relationship to the law, and we are now going to talk them out of existence by establishing the right relationship. By knowing a greater good, we are going to *un*know what we have known to our hut.

Very simply stated, the process is that of removing power from evil causes by transferring power to good causes. "Power belongeth unto God" said St. Paul. There is only One Power, and the only way to use It is through the creative process of man's thought. Yes, man has the sole responsibility for directing this undifferentiated power through his own thought. He can do with It what he will; he can built health of sickness, success or failure, happiness or sorrow.

The real solution to the problem of evil, therefore, is in keeping the power flowing toward Good. How shall we do that? By walling off every vestige of the human mind that believes in duality (good and evil), and by living by indirection like the birds of the air and the lilies of the field. In other words, we shall stop thinking by our own volition and think by the volition of God We shall not only cast "down imaginations . . . and bring into captivity every thought to the obedience of Christ," but we shall keep only constructive, positive, and life-giving thoughts flowing through our minds. Realizing our failure to bring out anything good through human thinking, we shall live by unthinking— that is, without effort, anxiety, or strain. We shall refuse to turn our thought outward toward the senses, opinions, theories, or doctrines of men; we shall behold the Kingdom of God in all its beauty and loveliness. But what of the human mind? That will go on thinking just the same, but God will think through it. Like the unthinking lobster that grows a new claw whenever he needs one, we shall have every need supplied automatically. When? When we become unthinkers—when we let God do our thinking for us and meet every demand of the outer world by saying to ourselves, "Be still, and now that I am God."

WHAT I CAN DO WITH ME

"If two of you shall agree as touching anything they shall ask, it shall be done for them of my Father." MATT. 18:19

The reason you can talk with yourself is because there are two of you — an inner man and an outer man, a spiritual man and a material man, an *I* and a *me*. Welded together in a union from which there is no escape, the two selves forever keep one from running away from himself, for the *I* always follows and catches up with the *me*.

One of the greatest problems we all have to face is how *I* can live harmoniously and successfully with *me* — how *I* can come to terms with *myself*. All achievement on the outer plane depends upon the individual's success in synchronizing the two selves. If *I* and *me* are not in perfect agreement, discord and unhappiness appear. If *I* and *me* are pulling in opposite directions, there is no centrality or direction in one's life; he is at the mercy of every wind that blows.

Psychiatrists recognize the danger of disintegration. The victim of a split personality is powerless against the demands of the objective world. Until harmony is restored within, there can be no semblance of peace and security in his environment. On the contrary, the man who has established peace within himself, whose life is unified or integrated, can meet danger and disaster triumphantly.

Let us turn to the Scriptures to see what *I* can do with *me*. St. Paul says, "Put off the old man [me] and put on the new man [I] which is Christ;" and Jesus said, "I, if I be lifted up will draw all men [manifestation] unto me." In other words, we must think and live outside ourselves by thinking and living

8

with God. One who is tired of strain, sickness, trouble, and limitation can be born anew by keeping the *I* and the *me* in perfect agreement with God, by telling himself constantly that this unity has been achieved, and by living as if it were so. So said St. Paul: "I live, yet not I but Christ liveth in me."

Robert A. Russell

CHAPTER 2

WHERE DO YOUR TROUBLES COME FROM?

Probably the most puzzling and distressing of all human problems is the problem of evil and sin. What is this false affirmer that prevents us from realizing the power of good in our lives? What is this sorcery that overlays our perfection with imperfection, our health with sickness, our supply with limitation, our fortune with misfortune, our peace with discord, and our happiness with misery? What is this devil that bedevils us, this witch that bewitches us, the sin which besets us, and this satanic power which confuses us? Why is it that when I would do good I do evil? And what is this evil that seems to challenge the very Presence and Power of God? Where did all this chaos, confusion, and trouble come from? If God is all and is Good, then how can evil exist? If God is Power and omnipresent, how can evil have more power than good? How can an All-Wise, All-Loving, All-Knowing, All-Powerful, and Ever-Present Deity be set in opposition to Himself? If God is Perfect and if we are made in His image and likeness, how does all this imperfection get into our lives?

The answers to these questions are all found in the story of "The Temptation and Fall of Man" in the Garden of Eden. To understand the lesson in this story, you must first understand the meaning of the symbols back of it. The garden represents the highest state of spiritual perfection, wholeness, and completion, called in the Bible the Kingdom of Heaven. The plants in the garden represent man's thoughts and ideas. The two trees growing in the center represent the Tree of Life and the tree of the knowledge of good and evil. They are placed in the center of the garden because man's life and consciousness are not only built around them but are fixed by them. They form the center from which all human experience springs. Eve represents the soul or consciousness; Adam symbolizes the physical body. Adam means "red clay" — the soma or earth principle.

Before Adam and Eve fell (ate of the tree of the knowledge of good and evil and divided their thought), they lived in a state of absolute perfection. After they fell, they were cast into a state of separation which, in the Bible, is a consciousness or knowledge of good and evil. The deception that brings all trouble into our lives is an inverted and perverted sense of life. It is an abuse of the creative faculty of thought.

WHY DID MAN FALL?

If you will think of the Garden of Eden as symbolic of the soul, and of the man and woman as symbolic of the mind and body, you will see that the "Fall" referred to is an ever-recurring experience in the life of man. The characters in this drama are a husband and wife (Adam and Eve) and a tempter, designated as a serpent. The scene is a lush garden in the Nile valley and the props are two trees — the tree of Life and the tree of the knowledge of good and evil. The plot is concerned with the man and wife who are so inextricably bound together that when the woman is tempted and falls, the husband falls with her. There is nothing in the story to indicate that the husband was tempted, but he went down just the same.

One wonders as he reads this story if Moses ever got the inner meaning of it over to his people. Cleverly, he clothed his words in symbols. If they obeyed the symbols, he knew they would get the same results as if they understood the law back of them.

The story of Adam and Eve is a convincing picture of the reciprocal action between the mind and body. The body is but a mirror of the mind. Body and mind are two ends of the same thing—man. They act and react reciprocally, never independently. What affects the mind affects the body. What the mind does, the body does with it. If the mind is tempted, the body is tempted. If the mind falls, the body falls. Where does the serpent come in? The serpent is the carnal mind—the belief in evil; it represents the thought turned down toward sense or experience. It causes man to judge according to appearances and from purely fleshly or human standards. The serpent says "Cancer is incurable," "This is impossible," or "That is insurmountable," despite the fact that the words are proved false every day. The great curse before which man falls is the belief in duality (the knowledge of good and evil).

This belief in separation from God is the source of all our griefs, woes, and illnesses. Had Adam and Eve (body and mind) not broken the law, the harmony in which our souls were created would never have been disturbed.

WHY DID TROUBLE COME TO YOU?

Let us consider now the *why* of evil. Why did evil come into your life and why is it perpetuated from day to day? You say that you never consciously thought of the particular difficulty from which you suffer. Perhaps not. But unwittingly you did think the things which brought the difficulty upon you. Since all evil is set in motion through wrong thinking, it could have come to you in but one of two ways: through your failure to comply with Divine Principle, or through ignorance. You attracted evil because you were subject to it, because you believed in it. It was the result of your belief in something apart from or greater than God; or conversely, your ignorance of the One God. Most errors imply lack; ignorance is a lack of knowledge of truth. Confusion indicates a lack of harmony; discord indicates a lack of peace; sickness indicates a lack of health; poverty indicates a lack of supply; and disorder indicates a lack of unity.

You can readily see that your troubles came upon you through the double-power doctrine and double vision. Instead of seeing with the single eye of Christ, you have seen with the double vision of the carnal mind. Thinking outside the principles of Truth, you have seen two powers instead of one, good and evil; two substances instead of one, Spirit and matter; two conditions instead of one, heaven and hell. The carnal conception of things is thus formed, and you begin to move out from wholeness into separation and adulteration. Believing that evil as well as good has a self-originating cause, you come into the consciousness of both good and evil, and trouble enters your life. In other words, you open a new window into your soul (create a new affinity). Where before there was only one window open to God, you now have another window open to evil. The first Guest is life-giving; the second guest is death-dealing. The first builds; the second destroys. Consciousness of Good causes you to see things right side up in relation to the Law of God; consciousness of evil makes you see things up side down in their relation to "the law of sin and death." The fall of man is repeated every time you accept the false testimony of the carnal mind and allow it to control and dominate you. When the window is closed to evil, it will stop coming into your life. "To the pure thou wilt show thyself pure; to the froward thou wilt show thyself froward."

HOW DID YOUR TROUBLE COME?

When we realize that we and we alone are responsible for all the evil that enters our lives, we shall stop blaming God or others for our ills, troubles, failures, sorrows, and unhappiness. Evil comes to us in just one way and operates in just one way — through suggestion, acceptance, and belief. In the twenty-eighth chapter of Deuteronomy, we read: "The Lord shall cause thine enemies to rise up against thee to be smitten before thy face: for they shall come out against thee one way and flee before thee seven ways." Most of us are aware of evil only after it has taken possession of us; very few know how it comes. When the method it uses is perceived, however, the problem of handling and overcoming it will be simple.

Let us approach the problem with this thought in mind: Evil comes to us as suggestion and operates through our belief. Evil is not person, place, or thing. It is an impersonal thought operating through our consciousness. The belief in evil is the only evil there is. If we accept the suggestion of evil (react positively to a negative), it moves into our consciousness and begins to express itself in our lives. It has an affinity, so to speak, for other evils; and it will permeate, contaminate, and discolor our entire experience if allowed to remain. If, on the other hand, we refuse to accept the suggestion of evil (refuse to respond to it, entertain it, or give it power), it will die for lack of recognition or attention.

But evil, no matter how hideous its form, is powerless unless we furnish it a belief or body to act through. It comes to us for power, substance, and life, and we give it all the power, substance, and life that it has. No matter what form the particular suggestion of evil may take — fear, worry, hate, resentment, doubt, sickness, or poverty, it cannot live without a mind and body to act through. It dies by inanition. It falls by its own weight. If we do not give brains, faculties, emotions, and physical organs to evil to act with, it will disappear and let us alone. In other words, evil cannot come to us unless we accept it. Being nothing and being recognized as such, it can do nothing. We render it powerless when we recognize and declare its nothingness.

WHAT CAN YOU DO ABOUT TROUBLE?

Since the human (carnal) mind is filled with many impurities, it is incapable of thinking straight, or according to Truth. It thinks from the standpoint of evil, weakness, and lack instead of from the standpoint of good, power, and plenty. St. Paul said, "The carnal mind is not subject to the law of God, Neither indeed can it be. To be carnally minded is death [having things in reverse — sickness, discord, poverty, failure and lack]; to be spiritually minded is life and peace [health, harmony, plenty, success]." In order to overcome evil, we must learn to reverse our thoughts and to think from the standpoint of the Christ Mind instead of from that of the human mind.

The usual approach to the solution of personal difficulties is by the labored and frantic activity of the human mind; the true method is by the unlabored and involuntary motion of the Christ Mind. Meeting defeat in one direction, the human mind turns in another. But no matter how or where it turns, there is no solution or escape. Why not? Because "the carnal mind is enmity against God." In spite of this revelation, man goes on trying to gain dominion over evil with a mind that is basically evil. It doesn't make any difference what a man thinks or what he strives to do; if he acts from the standpoint of personality, he is calling the human mind into action and increasing his trouble.

The true way to overcome evil and trouble is to turn entirely away from appearance, still the mind, and establish one's self in the Mind of Christ with this thoughts: BECAUSE ALL GOD'S WISDOM IS MINE, I AM NOW DIRECTED AND GUIDED IN ALL MY AFFAIRS, AND I AM DELIVERED OUT OF MY TROUBLES. Then keep the mind quietly centered in God; make no effort to solve or change the problem by the wisdom and methods of the human mind. If we let that Mind be in us which was also in Christ Jesus, it will dispose of trouble by giving us something good in its place. It will give us spiritual life instead of material life. It will give us peace instead of discord. It will give us health instead of sickness. It will establish us in the Kingdom of God.

WHAT IS THE CAUSE OF SICKNESS?

"Power belongeth unto God." Ps. 62:11

The only reason anyone ever becomes sick is that he thinks of himself as "two beings and two bodies" instead of one. When Jesus said, "Physician, heal thyself," He was not talking to those who were still in the fleshly consciousness but to those who were in spiritual consciousness, to those who represented the perfect unity between God and man. In the old forms of religion, we had the same problem — God and man, God and devil, Good and evil, Heaven and hell, Health and sickness, Life and death. There were always two instead of one — always God and something else. Out of this warfare between opposites have come all the suffering, ills, and limitations of man.

Jesus did not say, "I and the Father are *two*," or *"four"*, or *"six,"* but "I and the Father are one." *I am. You are.* That is enough. Just us the principle of mathematics is always one with its numerals, you and I are one with the Principle or Truth of God. Did not St. Paul tell us that "when Christ, Who is our Life, shall appear, then shall ye also appear with Him in glory?" What did he mean? He meant that when we have unified ourselves with God (knowing no other and giving power to no other), we "shall also appear in glory," for we shall see ourselves as we are in Reality (perfect). In other words, we shall think of ourselves not as a material body, subject to sin, sickness, and death but as the perfect body of God. This is the Truth that Jesus said would enable us to overcome conditions and transcend the world.

Again St. Paul said, "Ye are the wisdom, knowledge, and power of God." Let us start to claim this power by acting out our unity with God. The only reason a poultice or shot in the arm works more quickly and effectively than a metaphysical treatment is that material remedies are more real to our consciousness than spiritual treatments. In the fleshly mind, it is much easier to believe in matter than in Spirit. But in either case, the essential elements are belief and faith. All healing is based on the recognition of the power of God. A pill or a poultice is a step in this direction. Let us be satisfied (until we see ourselves differently) to demonstrate what we are.

CHAPTER 3

THE LAST COMING

"Lo, I am with you always, even unto the end of the world,"
MATT. 28:20.

Whether or not God words in our behalf and responds to our calls depends upon whether we have a present realization of His Presence or a future hope; whether we believe that Christ is already here or that He is still in a delayed state of coming; whether we believe that our salvation and needs are met in the Christ Nature which Jesus possessed, or in the personality of the man Jesus.

Jesus said: "God IS Spirit, and they that worship Him must worship Him in spirit and in Truth." How can an all-pervading, omnipresent Spirit be in some distant time or place? How can that which is "nearer — than breathing and closer than hands and feet" be in a state of evolution? How can a man of flesh and blood occupy and permeate a Universe that is essentially Spiritual? How can one contact the Divine Spirit except through the Spirit of his own mind and through his realization that It is already here?

Let those who still look for the first Advent answer these question. Let them tell us what the Christian world could have done these two thousand years without the Christ Presence. Let them explain what happened at Pentecost. Let them explain what happened at Pentecost, the rending of the veil of the temple (the removal of barriers between man and his God), the seven-branched golden candlesticks of the book of Revelation, and the many unmistakable statements that Christ is among His people. Let those who still look for the second Advent explain the words of Jesus, "Lo, I am with you always," and St. Paul's phrase, "Christ in you, the hope of glory." Don't you see how those still looking for the second coming have missed the event and are delaying their good?

The first coming of Jesus as revealed in the Scriptures was Immanuel—*God with us.* The second coming was *God within Us.* The first was the Divine word made flesh. The second was the Divine word made Spirit. Jesus said: "If I [the physical man] go not away, the Holy Comforter [Spirit] will not come unto you." Thus Jesus took His fleshly body out of the here into the everywhere in order that His Spirit might be instantly and constantly available to all men.

The Spirit comes through a deep realization of its Presence within ourselves and not through observation or by searching. No longer limited to Galilee in physical form, He is now unlimited in every soul.

SPIRITUAL TREATMENT

"Ye shall know the Truth, and the Truth shall make you free." JOHN 8:32.

A metaphysical treatment given on the spiritual plane is just as definite a thing as medicine administered on the physical plane. In reality , they are two ends of the same thing, for both provide means through which the Healing Principle can operate. One works from center (Source of Life) out to the circumference of the body; the other works from the circumference in toward the soul. One works from the spiritual to the material; the other works from the material to the spiritual. One words through cause; the other, through effect. One works through God; the other, through man. One employs Divine Intelligence; the other employs the natural forces of the body.

The real difference between the two methods obviously is not in the Principle employed but in the power upon which faith is centered. In the first method, faith comes from the knowledge of man's unity with God and his consequent right to wholeness and harmony. In the second method, faith is centered in the skill of the physician and in minerals, vitamins, and drugs.

Spiritual treatment is a definite movement of God's Mind to a specific person for a specific need, as a result of the realization on the part of the healer that the word he speaks contains within itself sufficient power and intelligence to demonstrate itself. It is speaking the authoritative word embodying the Truth belied by the specific appearance occasioning the treatment. It is more than wishing or hoping something good may happen. It is knowing that it has already happened.

"The Kingdom of Heaven *is* at hand." The good we seek is already here; it has always been here. Health is ours. Supply is ours. Peace is ours. Happiness is ours. How shall we appropriate these blessings? By RECOGNITION (knowing the Truth) and by ACCEPTANCE (embodying It in our daily lives). We receive only to the extend that we realize the Good that surrounds us and are aware of our relationship to it.

WHAT IS IT THAT HEALS?

Some say it is the power of mind over matter that heals, others that it is suggestion, others that it is magnetism, and still others that it is "The Father Within." We affirm the last because it is both Scriptural and Christian. Jesus did not begin his healing with heart trouble, tumors, flu, polio, crippled limbs, and deaf ears, but with "The Father Within," or the Principle of Life in His own Mind. His mighty formula was *health through unity with God*. His master principle was faith and prayer, and His great emphasis was upon the spiritualization of the individual mind.

God has not provided that there shall be no sickness, but that sickness, if it come, shall be overcome through cooperation with the Father Who makes a perfect balance of body, soul, and spirit. God did not intend that man should deteriorate and die of disease. E. L. House says, "The body might just wear out and pass away as naturally as the apple ripens and falls in the autumn, or the wheat matures and dies in June. 'Thou shalt come to thy grave in full age like as a shock or corn cometh in his season.' This is very different from the apple falling in June, with a worm in it. This is disease. The promise of spiritual healing is not physical immortality but health until our life work is done." Every sick person has in some way broken the connection with his Source. The natural condition of the body is health and wholeness; to recover these, one who is ill must, like the prodigal son, return to the consciousness of his oneness with God.

We find the answer to our question in an inscription over the entrance to a great hospital: "I bound up his wounds, but God healed him." All that the doctor or spiritual healer does is to stir up, or awaken, the divinity within; God does the rest. The same Divine Life that created the body also sustains and heals the body. It is the same power that rushes to our aid in every emergency, uniting broken bones, healing cuts and wounds, and supplying our daily needs.

ORTHODOX PRAYER AND METAPHYSICAL TREATMENT

The difference between an orthodox prayer and a metaphysical treatment is in the consciousness or the understanding of the one making it and not in the prayer, or treatment.

The Standard Dictionary defines prayer as "The art of offering reverent petitions to a divinity; the act of beseeching earnestly; a request for relief by complainant." Webster defines it as "Beseeching; earnest request or entreaty; petition; supplication; act of addressing supplication to a divinity or object of worship." These definitions clearly indicate the attitude of the orthodox mind in prayer as it attempts to force something from God that He is withholding or apparently unwilling to share. This God is far off, and the petitioner is an outcast. He is a worm of the dust, secondary to everything, filled with sin, mortality, and uncertainty.

A metaphysical treatment on the other hand recognizes God as the source of All Good—Good which is not only immediately responsive to our call but which is constantly seeking avenues of expression in and through us. The difference between the two prayers is in the degree of comprehension and understanding of the pray-er. The first prays to an unknown God in the future; the second accepts Him as a present Reality. The first widens the gap between the petitioner and God by an admission of incompleteness. The second closes the gap by the recognition and acceptance of that which is already his.

Jesus said, "Whatsoever things ye desire, when ye pray believe that ye have received them and ye shall have them." In other words, pray for what you believe you have instead of for what you believe you do not have. What is involved will evolve. If the Kingdom of God is within man and if God is present in that Kingdom, as Jesus said, there is also present within that Kingdom anything and everything man could possibly wish or ask for. If God is Omnipresent, as the Bible states, man can contact Him whenever and wherever he consciously recognizes and accepts his Presence.

Countless natural and scientific laws exist which do not affect the life of man because he does not make use of them. Any law of itself is futile. In order to operate, it must be specialized through man's thought; the individual must consciously impress upon the subconscious mind such desires as he wishes to see fulfilled. The subconscious mind in turn will cause them to materialize.

MEDICAL SCIENCE VERSUS METAPHYSICAL SCIENCE

When Truth students realize that medical science and metaphysical science depend upon the same Principle and that the most either one can do is to assist the patient's faith to assert itself, they will lose the sense of frustration and disappointment so often accompanying the failure to heal or to be healed through spiritual means. It is not he change in method or means that should concern us but the direction of our faith and the human tendency to mistake the means for the end. Means, let us remember, are simply agencies in which to center our faith. They are the outward and visible signs of an inward and Spiritual Grace; they have only the effect which the mind expects them to produce. When we have purified our consciousness to such an extent that it no longer takes account of sickness and disease, we shall do away with the means altogether. We shall not need outside help at all.

"There is therefore now on condemnation to them which are in Christ Jesus, who walk not after the flesh but after the spirit." Let us be sensible in such a matter, and not try to go beyond our mental equivalents. Let us not expect perfection until we are wholly in It. Let us not expect complete healing until we have the mind of Christ. Let us now hesitate to go to a doctor if we need one. If God is all and He is everywhere equally present, as Jesus said, we can cooperate as wholeheartedly and loyally with the medical practitioner as with the metaphysical practitioner, for we can work with both the material and the spiritual at the same time. In either case, it is God and our faith that do the healing, and there can be no self-condemnation where all the power and the glory are given to Him. There are good doctors and bad ones, just as there are good metaphysicians and poor ones. The good work with cause, and the poor with effects. The good treat the man, and the poor treat the disease.

This whole problem can be rationalized and met by realizing that all means are merely avenues through which God moves and by recognizing that we are always dependent upon the Grace of God and are never at any time dependent upon doctors or metaphysical.

CHAPTER 4

MECHANICS OF A TREATMENT

"Whatsoever a man soweth, that shall be also reap." GAL. 6:7

If I drop an object from my hand, it falls to the ground. Why does it fall? Why doesn't it go up in the air or in some other direction? The law of gravity controls it; it cannot work in any other way. The Law of Mind, too, is mechanical in its action. It doesn't think, choose, or decide; it only acts. It doesn't know good and evil, rich and poor, peace and discord, health and sickness. It accepts each one of us at our own estimate or evaluation of ourselves. Its response is determined by our plane of thought and quality of consciousness.

Just as water always seeks its own level and the angles of any triangle always add up to 180 degrees, the Creative Mind always gives back to us whatever we think into It, or whatever is embodied within our thoughts and words. If we plant radishes in the creative medium of the soil, we get back radishes and not onions. If we sow ideas of health in the Great Creative Mind of the Universe, we get back health and not sickness. The result is according to law, "For whatsoever a man soweth that shall be also reap."

Knowing this undeviating law gives us faith in our prayers and treatments. We know that they enter into us or into those for whom they were created in such degree as we comprehend or embody them in our words. "So shall my word be that goeth forth out of my mouth. It shall not return unto me void but shall accomplish that whereunto it is sent." Because the law works the way it does and never works in any other way, we can give a scientific treatment and be assured of a perfect outcome or revelation of the self to the self.

A treatment once given belongs to God; it is thenceforth out of personal hands. It has become an impersonal, mechanical, subjective thing, acted upon by Mind and operating in accordance with spiritual law. It is consciously given and becomes subjectively effective. It is given by the healer and becomes the property of the one toward whom it is directed. It knows nothing but that which we have put into it; its only purpose is to express that for which it was made. The rest of the process is simply an unswerving, living, and active faith in the efficacy of the treatment we have given.

STEPS IN GIVING A TREATMENT

The first step in giving a good treatment is to change the subjective trend. We act within ourselves to remove from our minds any belief in sickness, limitation, or imperfection. We neutralize the imperfect subjective patterns of disease and then substitute the more truthful and perfect patterns of health. In other words, we nullify (negate) the physical manifestation of disease by a greater realization of health. The metaphysical calls this process separating the belief from the believer.

Disease, like any other form of evil, is not person, place, or thing. It isn't an entity; it has no power of its own. It is merely a negative impersonal thought operating through the mind. The power of evil and disease comes from our attention, fear, and belief. When the attention, fear, and belief are removed, the disease disappears. How does one do that? By refusing to give disease a body to act with, eyes to see with, ears to hear with, emotions to feel with, and a mind to think with.

The second step in giving a spiritual treatmen: is to supply the subjective equivalent, or spiritual prototype, of the thing or condition desired. A spiritual prototype is a definite statement of the truth about the person or condition mentioned in the treatment. Its sole purpose is to reverse the old disease thought pattern and to make room for a greater expression of the Life that is already at the center of the one being treated. Since God is Omnipresent, we do not have to provide ways for Him to get into people, but we must develop means for Him to get out. The spiritual prototype provides a greater outlet of Divine Life from the center to the circumference.

The treatment is given through the conscious mind but becomes effective in the subconscious mind. It is not "holding thoughts" or "willing things to happen." It is the silent contemplation of God at the point where sickness and trouble seem to be. It is calling the good (Reality) out of the bad (the temporal) and the desirable (Perfection) out of the undesirable (imperfection).

REPETITION IN TREATMENT

One of the much discussed subjects in metaphysical circles is, "How many times should the treatment be given?" The answer is "Until the work is done." Some healers get quick results from their treatments, but the majority of healers do not. Delays should not deter or discourage us, however, for the space between the prayer and the answer is no more than the time required to reach a point of agreement in our own mind. "Now is the accepted time." God is Responsive

Intelligence. God is Omniactive. It is done. If we had the vision, comprehension, illumination, and unshakable conviction that Jesus had, every demonstration would be instantaneous. We, too, could speak the word that nothing can stop.

The waiting period in every demonstration is determined by two things: the degree of understanding, comprehension, and realization of the healer and his ability to reach the subconscious mind and make a sufficiently deep impression upon it. If the impression is shallow as in the case of partial acceptance and realization, the time element will be drawn out. If it is deep as in the case of perfect agreement with the Principle, it will be instantaneous. But in either case, it is a matter of spiritual growth, practice, and unfoldment. We shall never go beyond our mental equivalents; we shall never demonstrate anything but our own consciousness.

Since we can expect every demonstration in the present moment, let us realize that all subsequent treatments on the same problems are but a continuation of the first. There is only one treatment in any claim; it should continue as long as treatment is needed. Repetition brings revelation.

What is this good thing you are trying to project into your own or another's experience? Can you visualize it? Is it clear to you? Get a clear picture of what you wish to objectify and contemplate it regularly. Go into the silence three times a day. Claim the perfect creation as your own. Mentally accept it and demand that your inner self give it to you. Then close your treatment with a mighty pean of praise and thanksgiving to God for bringing perfection within the reach of man.

REACHING A CONCLUSION

"Now when Solomon made an end of praying, the fire came down from Heaven." 2 CHRON. 7:1.

There are many important factors in giving an effective treatment but probably none is more important than the termination of the prayer. This is very pertinent problem for those who fail in their purpose. Treatments long drawn out or poorly formed and executed are like clouds without rain.

To be effective a treatment must fill three demands. It must be conscious. It must be positive. It must reach a complete conclusion. The compact whole then becomes a nucleus that attracts all the creative forces of Good. This process continues until there is an overt expression or manifestation that corresponds to the nucleus.

It is a wise person, therefore, who learns early in his experience when and how to let go and when and how to let God. "Now when Solomon made an end of praying, the fire came down from Heaven, and consumed the burnt offering and the sacrifices; and the glory of the Lords filled the house [filled Solomon's consciousness]." Giving a treatment without reaching a conclusion is futile. It is like trying to make bricks without straw or posting a letter without a stamp. It is like holding a fishing fly over the water without dropping it in; there is no point of contact with the water, and consequently, no fish. Where there is no contact with the law, there can be no manifestation. Solomon said, "Trust in the Lord [Law] with all thine heart [Mind]." In other words, release your treatment into Creative Activity by acceptance, forgetfulness, and detachment. Know, as Jesus did, that "It is done." Then have done with it.

Personal obligation ceases when we reach a complete conclusion in the treatment. "Of mine own self I can do nothing." "The Father within He doeth the works." Let go of the treatment by addressing the Inner Self in some such manner as this:

"Here, Subjective Mind, is my treatment, a perfect pattern and vehicle for you to work through. You are a willing and able servant, and you never make a mistake. You will carry out my orders to the letter. You are even now acting upon my instructions. God bless you for your help."

INSTANTANEOUS HEALING

"The fields . . . are white already to harvest." John 4:35. *"Now is the accepted time."* 2 Cor. 6:2.

There are two sides to the law of seed time and harvest. On the material side, things occur slowly or in sequence. We tend to think in terms of human experience, and results follow the pattern we establish. But Jesus revealed a new pattern. "Say not ye, There are yet four months, and then cometh the harvest? Behold, I say unto you, Lift up your eyes and look on the fields; for they are white already to harvest." On the spiritual plane, there is neither past nor future. Ideas are formed in the present; all good things are in instant fulfillment. Demonstration is instantaneous.

Now read our text again: "The fields are white already to harvest." The Kingdom of Heaven is finished, present, and within man now. God, Responsive Intelligence, is NOW — this moment. "Now is the accepted time." "Before they call I will answer." Then why do we have to wait on our demonstrations?

If the things we desire from God are in instant fulfillment, why are they so long in coming? Can it be due to some failure on the part of God? No! The failure is in ourselves. We have failed to cooperate sufficiently with the Spirit of God. We have not kept our thinking in accord with Truth. We have chosen to believe the human mind which lends itself to delay and limitation instead of the Christ Mind which is active and instant in expression.

"For he spake and it was done; he commanded and it stood fast." That instantaneous healings do occur at times no one will deny. Metaphysical history is full of them. But all healings and demonstrations are not instantaneous, for we have not incorporated the idea of immediacy in our consciousness. We still believe in time, growth, anticipation, struggle, delay, and limitation. Our words have no substance because we still pray in a divided mind. Our results are negative because we do not realize that we are dealing with Divine Mind and not the human mind. Our desires are unfulfilled because we still have more faith in matter than in Spirit. If instantaneous healings take place outside the time process, the way we get instant results is to think solely with the Spirit and to visualize our desires as already created in form.

THE PRAYER OF FAITH SHALL SAVE THE SICK

Compiled by Williston M. Ford

Healing is not mere relief from disease but a positive relation with Christ—realization of the Divine Life within. This awareness of the Presence will raise your whole being to a new level. Strong, true thoughts, or affirmation, will develop this new consciousness. Replace any thought of weakness by true thought of strength.

"Let the Weak say I am strong." Joel 3:10. "The Lord is the strength of my life." Ps. 27:1. "I can do all things through Christ who strengtheneth me." Phil. 4:13.

True faith will cause our good to draw nearer and nearer — happiness, health, strength, success, consciousness of God. "According to your faith be it unto you." "All things are possible to him that believeth." Dismissing weakness and sickness from my mind, I lay hold of the inexhaustible strength and life of God.

"I AM A CONSCIOUS CENTER of the One Life that is always creating, healing, blessing, perfecting. In this sense Christ lives within me."

"THE HEALING POWER OF CHRIST circulates through every artery of my body filling me with Divine Saving Health."

"GOD, OF WHOM MY LIFE IS PART as my finger is part of my hand, is filling me with increasing strength and peace, hour by hour."

"INFINITE LOVE FROM THE FATHER sheds a tender forthgiving spirit throughout my whole being—relieving all pain, tension, fretfulness."

Open to God every hour of the day. You cannot think of God too often. The continued sense of His Presence will give you an inner peace and joy. Replace, therefore, any thought of depression, irritation, or apprehension, with words like these:

"Thou hast put gladness into my heart." Ps. 4:7. "In Thy Presence is fulness of joy." Ps. 16:11. "Joy cometh in the morning." Ps. 30:5. "They joy of Christ is my joy; it is joy victorious, triumphant, overcoming."

Before welcoming sleep at night or during the day, repeat the following words slowly, breathing after each word: "I will give you rest." Mt. 11:28. "My peace I give unto you." Jn. 14:27. "Father, into Thy hands I commend my spirit." Lk. 23:46. "In quietness and confidence shall be your strength." Is. 30:15. "Thou wilt keep him in perfect peace whose mind is stayed on Thee." Is. 26:3. "Be still and know that I am God." Ps. 46:10. "Underneath are the everlasting arms." Deut. 33:27.

EVENING PRAYER

The day and the work God gave me are done; and now He has given me the night and beautiful rest. I trust myself, body and spirit, into His keeping through the mystery of sleep. I am God's child. As tides from the ocean fill the bay, so peace and strength and love fill my life to overflowing as I rest quietly in Him. Because I am God's child. I rest in Him—bravely, quietly, patiently, with confidence and self control.*

---

* *Used by permission of SHARING.*

Robert A. Russell

CHAPTER 5

SILENCE IN HEALING

"The Lord is in his Holy Temple; let all the earth keep silence before Him." HAB. 2:20.

There are many reasons why one should practice the silence at least twice a day. None is more important, however, than the sense of unity that entering the silence establishes with the Creator.

The dictionary defines the word *silence* as abstinence from noise, as stillness, poise, tranquility, serenity, and quiet. At the heart of every living thing is a great depth of stillness and quiet; to enter that stillness is to balance the body and mind and to lay hold of the power, peace, and substance of God. Automatically, you close the door of your mind to all outer confusion, disorder, and material claims—close it to everything that contradicts your unity and perfection in Christ.

To silence the mind and body while centering them in Spirit is to bring them into unity with God. To maintain the silence (carry it over into every day living) is to maintain health, power, and efficiency—to install insulation against the wear, tear, and friction of the world.

When you are silent in mind and body and are receptive towards God, every cell of the body receives the quickening, vitalizing, and healing power of His Love and Wholeness. Then each organ and each function work in perfect rhythm and harmony with every other organ and function. You become a distributor and generator of Divine Health and Wholeness. You become divinely pregnant.

How do you enter the silence? Sit or lie in a state of absolute mental and physical relaxation. Do this at least twice daily, the first thing upon awakening in the morning, and just before retiring at night. First, choose a short but meaningful affirmation such as, "My soul, wait thou in silence for God only; for my expectation is from Him." (Use it again at the close of your silence to furnish the element on which the Creative Powers of the mind are to work).

Then meditate upon your affirmation. "It is the Spirit that quickeneth." Get into the Spirit of it. Feel the Truth of it. Relax and let go a little more.

You will know by your sense of well-being when your contact with the Inner Self has been established. Conclude your silence with your original affirmation. Thank God for the fulfillment of your desires and go on your way with the sure confidence that you have been made whole—that God is directing your every step and that He is supplying you with your highest good.

BOLDNESS IN SPIRITUAL HEALING

"Now when they saw the boldness of Peter and John, and perceived that they were unlearned and ignorant men, they marvelled; and they took knowledge of them that they had been with Jesus." ACTS 4:13.

Just as faith heart never wins fair lady, feeble demands upon the Law never bring out the maximum power and action of

God. The greatest hindrances to an immediate and abundant response from the Universal Mind are limp thinking, a divided mind, double vision, broken loyalties, weak assumptions, infirm purposes, watered faith, and adulterated thoughts. Spiritual boldness and certitude come from an intimate association and fellowship with Christ. Without this association, we are like Simon Peter in the mud state— impetuous, impulsive, as the mud becomes rock (Petros) under the influence of a fierce and consuming affection. In the mud stage, he denied his Lord three times: yielding, indecisive, and uncertain. But see him "I know not that man." In the rock stage, he performed a miraculous healing and preached a sermon that added five thousand men to the church.

What was the secret of this great transformation wherein plastic mud became irresistible rock? We find the answer in the eighth verse of the fourth chapter of Acts: "Then Peter filled with the Holy Ghost." This boldness was not the product of education, erudition, or special leaning, for " they were unlearned and ignorant men." It was an unseen and Unconditioned Power behind Peter and John that gave them this force. It was St. Peter plus Christ. It was St. John plus God.

But why marvel at the certitude and boldness of Peter and John? Why do we not cultivate this same aggressiveness and confidence for ourselves? Why not let this same Mind, Holy Spirit, and Divine Energy be in us? This spiritual boldness is the imperative need of every treatment; it is the guarantee of success. We need men and women today who take God at His Word, who pray "nothing doubting," who believe that their word is powerful enough to penetrate and dispel every inharmonious condition, and who believe that with God all things are possible.

PRAYER FOR SPIRITUAL BOLDNESS

"And now, Lord, behold their threatenings, and grant unto thy servants that with all boldness, they may speak Thy Word, by stretching forth Thy hand to heal, and that signs and wonders may be cone by the Name of Thy Holy Child, Jesus."

PERSISTENCE IN HEALING

What miracles persistency performs! When material means have dried up, medical genius has failed, and the surgeon has quit, when courage surrenders and hope flees, when every door is closed and all human agencies have retired, then faith and persistency do the impossible. The last to leave the sick room, the last to turn back, the last to take *no* for an answer, persistence wins out when everything else has failed.

Probably the most striking example of the virtue of persistence in spiritual work is to be found in the Syro-Phoenician woman's triumph over the opposition and seeming apathy of Jesus toward her request that He heal her child. "Have mercy on me, O Lord, Thou Son of David," she cried. St. Matthew says that "He answered her not a word." Why didn't He answer her and what hope could she have when even the disciples were arrayed against her? We read: "His disciples besought Him saying, Send her away for she crieth after us."

It is hard to imagine a more disappointing and discouraging situation. But this woman was not to be defeated; she would not take no for an answer. Then comes the change in the situation; Jesus breaks His silence and addresses her as a gentile. "I am not sent but unto the lost sheep of the House of Israel." This would have been enough for most people, but outcast though she was, she would not give up. Instead of being deterred by His words, she throws herself at His feet and cries, "Lord, help me." But Jesus had still another test to put upon her faith. "It is not meet to take the children's bread and to cast it to dogs." What a blow that must have been and yet how wonderfully she met it! Listen to the genius of her reply and realize the dauntlessness of her faith: "Truth, Lord, yet the dogs eat the crumbs that fall from the master's table." That did it. Jesus was so impressed and overcome by her faith and persistency that He cried out with exultant joy: "O woman, great is thy faith: be it unto thee even as thou wilt." And St. Matthew tells us that "her daughter was made whole from that very hour."

Now what does this lesson teach? It teaches that opposition clarifies and strengthens faith when it is rightly met. Jesus took the woman's little faith and increased it until it was adequate for the healing of her daughter. When obstacles become a stimulus to faith, there is nothing that cannot be healed.

REALIZATION IN HEALING

"He that cometh to God must believe that He is, and that He is a rewarder of them that diligently seek him." Heb. 11:6.

When the metaphysician speaks of realization in treatment, he means the objectification or materialization of the thing asked for. It is an attitude of mind that embodies completion, fulfillment, perfection, and wholeness. If it is directed toward God with the conviction that the need has already been met, it becomes the ability to do anything that needs to be done. The mind, however, must so completely accept the idea that contradiction or denial is impossible.

Jesus voiced this same truth in His statement: "HEAVEN AND EARTH SHALL PASS AWAY, BUT MY WORDS SHALL NOT PASS AWAY UNTIL ALL BE FULFILLED." That is what realization is. It is the inward assurance and conviction of the fulfillment and out-working of the treatment we have set in motion. Prayer that enters into realization always brings a demonstration. Are unrealized prayers then unanswered? Precisely! If a man prays for healing and cannot get beyond the appearance of disease, his prayer will have little or no effect. If he prays for supply and cannot rise above the thought of limitation, he will not get what he prays for.

We bring realization into our treatments and prayers by centering attention determinedly on the consummation of our desire until we have a realization, or, as Charles Filmore says, "until the idea, serving as a nucleus for similar ideas, has expanded to the point of potential action. When this realization is had, the metaphysician rests from all his work."

We must remember that all material objects were first ideas in mind, fashioned by the imagination from God's omnipresent thought substance and set in motion through acceptance, faith, and fixity of vision. First, the mind conceives an idea; then through realization, it concentrates all its forces to give that idea form in the outer world.

In the old Sanskrit, the word *real* means "from thought-to-thing." Thus, realization is the process through which thoughts, desires, and decrees become things. First, you conceive what you want and make a clear, definite, and perfect picture of it in your mind. Then you hold it lovingly in your heart as a mother loves her child. You give it power through faith, integration through unification, form through meditation, action through acceptance, materialization through surrender and forgetfulness, and fulfillment through praise and thanksgiving.

CHAPTER 6

PRAISE IN HEALING

"But I . . . will praise thee more and more." Ps. 71:14.

"There is an inherent law of mind that we increase whatever we praise. The whole of creation responds to praise and is glad. Animal trainers pet and reward their charges with delicacies for acts of obedience; children glow with joy and gladness when they are praised. Even vegetation grows better for those who love it. We can praise our own ability, and the very brain cells will expand and increase in capacity and intelligence when we speak words of encouragement and appreciation to them.

"A farmer and his wife in South Dakota during the drouth period praised each furrow plowed and blessed every seed; they secured abundant crops, when their neighbors obtained none.

"H. K. Mozumdar of Hollywood tested the principle of praise on two rose bushes. For two weeks, he daily praised one and cursed the other. Growing conditions were the same in each case, but while one blossomed beautifully, the other died.

"Mozumdar himself, when an octogenarian, looked like a youth of thirty. He gave credit for his youthful appearance to his habit of praising his body and giving thanks to God daily. The doctors told Brown Landone at fifty that he had better put his affairs in order as his heart was giving out. Instead, he spent a part of every day praising the cells of his heart and body, and at ninety he often worked twenty-four hours of the twenty-four without fatigue."*

How can we focus this gigantic principle upon our bodily powers and cause them to work in harmony with God's Law of Perfect Health to secure the higher vitality of the body temple? By expanding and nourishing the health we already have. We do this by daily blessing and praising the functions, organs, and cells of the body until they are alive and vibrating with the Presence and Power of God. Praise not only builds health in the body but carries away all the accumulated debris of negative and erroneous thinking. It is the secret of eliminating pain and the solvent for trouble in the mind. God has given us the power to praise, and every man must utilize this power for himself. Praise is the sure way of opening the whole being to God and of appropriating His rich blessings of Spiritual health.

THANKSGIVING IN HEALING

"In everything by prayer and supplication with thanksgiving let your requests be made unto God." PHIL. 4:6.

Probably the most striking lesson that Jesus drew on the value and importance of thanksgiving in healing was in the story of the ten lepers. He was on His way to Jerusalem when He met ten lepers "who stood afar off." Seeing our Lord, they cried out saying: "Jesus, Master, have mercy on us." There was an instant cleansing in Jesus' response, for He told them to go and show themselves to the priests or health officers of that day. After they had been restored to their position among normal people, one of them (a Samaritan) returned to give

---

* *Wanvig, Orlando. Quoted by permission.*

thanks. Jesus amazed asked: "Were not ten cleansed? But where are the nine?" Then to the Samaritan, Jesus imparted a special and richer blessing: "Arise, go thy way; thy faith hath made thee whole."

The special and richer blessing received by the Samaritan went beyond the boundaries of physical healing. He was made *whole*, and *wholeness* implies that he had achieved a state of unity — unity of the body, soul, and spirit. The nine who were healed in body had taken a step toward wholeness; their future depended upon their success in building upon this one phase. But the Samaritan had indeed been blessed. His growth was assured by his gesture of thanksgiving. The simple act of expressing gratitude became a permanent connection with the Source of Being.

"Don Blanding tells of an Hawaiian boy who became wealthy. He pasted over his bed the words, 'LORD, I DO GIVE THEE THANKS FOR THE ABUNDANCE THAT IS MINE,' which he repeated many times daily. In the Bible, Paul and Silas were thrown into prison; instead of repining, they sang songs of praise and thanksgiving, and the prison walls were shaken down. Twice Jesus looked from a few paltry baskets of fish and bread to hungry thousands, gave thanks for what He had and praised it, and then fed the multitude with a surplus.

"God gave man dominion over the earth and all it contains. As to Adam He brought every living creature to be named, so likewise He presents you with every possible situation; you may call it good or bad, but whatever you call it so it becomes to you. Call it good and praise it with thanksgiving and it will increase as good, for only the good, the positive, can grow; evil is negation and is dissolved."

LOVE IN HEALING

"Thou shalt love the Lord thy God with all thy heart, and with all thy soul, and with all thy strength, and with all thy mind; and thy neighbor as thyself." LUKE 10:27.

It is safe to say that if we loved God and our neighbor as Jesus directed, there would never be any sickness, disease, dislocation, or impoverishment in our lives. "Love . . . seeketh not its own; is not puffed up." Love is not self-centered. We cannot have love and sickness at the same time. We cannot be in unity with God unless we love everybody; we must love our neighbor as we do ourselves because we are all one.

Are things going badly with you? Are your problems almost more than you can bear? Are you tried to the limit? Is your life disrupted and are your forces crippled? Are you out of sorts with yourself and are others out of sorts with you? Is your spirit embittered? Then there is but one thing to do: PUT YOURSELF IN THE WAY OF BEING FOUND BY GOD.

There problems are only secondary; the primary problem is yourself. It is easy to blame the world, other individuals, or unfavorable circumstances. Instead, the blame rests within. The source of all human problems is a selfish, unloving, dislocated, and unfocused self. What we lump together as unfavorable circumstances is nothing more or less than the result of distorted and decentralized thinking. To better our conditions and circumstances, we must change the self back again to the center.

When Nicodemus came to Jesus asking what he must do to inherit eternal life, Jesus said; "Thou shalt love the Lord thy God with all thy heart, and with all thy soul, and with all thy strength, and with all thy mind." Fulfilling this requirement is the only way to open life so that we can receive power. Life to be strong and well-balanced must have both an inlet and an outlet—must be open at both ends.

Is that all? No, "Thou shalt love thy neighbor as thyself"—not more nor less than yourself but as yourself. You shall love God, your neighbor, and yourself with all your strength, with all your mind, all your soul, and all your body. Do you see Jesus' point? By loving God with your whole being, you open the inlet, and by loving your neighbor in the same way, you provide the outlet. When the flow has been balanced between inlet and outlet, you will have removed all tensions and obstructions from your life.

FORGIVENESS AND HEALING

Since the body has been formed by thought and feeling, as science has proved, it can be re-formed by new thoughts and new feelings patterned after the Spiritual Body of our Christ Nature. Ultimately, the outer body will be mental, not material, for it is an aggregation of thought structures, or ways of thinking.

How shall we proceed to re-form the body according to our Divine Nature? There are two ways: by forgiveness and by repentance. "All sin," Charles Fillmore says, "is first in the mind; and forgiveness is a change of mind, or repentance. Some mental attitude, some train of mental energy, must be transformed. We forgive sin every time we resolve to think and act according to Divine Law. The mind must change from a material to a spiritual base. The Law is already fixed; there is nothing in it to be changed, because God is the lawgiver and does not change. The change must be on the part of man and within him. The moment man changes his thoughts of sickness to thoughts of health, the Divine Law rushes in and begins the healing work."

In his words to the paralytic, Jesus shows us the intimate relationship between sin and disease and the therapeutic value of forgiveness and repentance. The first step toward healing and normal health is forgiveness, or removal of the cause. "If we confess our sins, God is faithful and just to forgive us our sin, and to cleanse us from all unrighteousness." The second step is repentance, the turning of the mind toward God and away from self. Forgiveness and healing go hand in hand. When Jesus gave His Apostles the command to heal the sick, He also gave them the authority to forgive sin.

Let us remember that we shall never rise higher than we lift ourselves and others in our thought. If we would be free and whole, we must keep our mental systems clean by daily forgiving ourselves and others for everything.

"But that ye may know that the Son of man hath authority on earth to forgive sins [he said unto him that was palsied], I say unto thee, Arise, and take up thy bed, and go unto thy house. And immediately he rose up before them, and took up that whereon he lay, and departed to his house, glorifying God."

"Receive ye the Holy Ghost; whose soever sins ye remit, they are remitted unto them; and whose soever sins ye retain, they are retained." Sickness is a manifestation of maladjustment— an indication that one's consciousness is out of alignment with the purpose and Will of God. Health results from the re-formation of the body under Spiritual Law.

CHAPTER 7

AGREE WITH EVIL QUICKLY

Jesus said, "Agree with thine adversary quickly whilst thou art in the way with him." The adversary referred to is any form of evil or negation that may be troublesome. Why are we not told to run far and fast to escape him? Why must we agree? Because by agreeing with evil, we obviate the necessity of having to handle it. How do we agree with an adversary? By seeing it as it is and by exposing it to the white light of Truth. Instead of fearing, resisting, and fighting evil as we have been doing, we now agree with it and render it powerless.

Our first step in this process is to examine evil and to see it for what it is. Evil is a false belief parading as the truth. It is a negation of the good. It is a false mental picture, generated and sustained by wrong or inverted thinking; it has no power to embody or to express itself. It is temporary because it disappears in the presence of Good. It us unreal because it is impermanent. Having no self-originating cause, it is merely an effect. It is not absolute because it exists only in the human or carnal mind and lives by borrowed life.

We must give the devil his due; evil does serve one useful purpose, however. It serves by creating in us a desire for the good. "On the one hand, evil is necessary for good, for were the imperfections not felt, there would be no striving for perfection. All defect and sin consist merely in privation, in the non-realization of possible qualities. It would not be well were evil non-existent, for it makes for the necessity of good;

49

if evil were removed, the desire for good would also cease. In its whole life, however, the soul will realize all good, and therefore is only *per accideus* imperfect."*

We shall agree with evil then by seeing it as a form of good. We shall transmute it by recognizing it as an inevitable step toward an expanding consciousness and an ever greater realization of God.

If evil is something out of which good is made, where is the evil? All life and energy are of divine origin; that which we name *evil* is merely unreconstructed energy. To gain this understanding and maintain it will save us from much unnecessary suffering and many mistakes. Instead of reacting unpleasantly to the negative things that happen to us, we shall see them as the best things that could have happened because they provide us with the opportunities to learn the wisdom that we need.

RESIST NOT EVIL

The way to overcome evil is not by fighting or resisting but by a radical change in consciousness. If man's viewpoint (belief) is the only evil there is, the belief in evil is the only thing that can be changed. "God hath made man perfect, but man hath sought out many inventions." He has resisted evil; and the more he has resisted, the stronger it has grown. He has fought evil; and by the reflex action of his own belief, it has fought back with equal force. Why? Because what man resists becomes real, and what is real to his consciousness becomes steadfast and indestructible. Evil is not real in the sense that good is real, but man invests it with reality by giving it power

* McIntyre, J. L. GIORDANO BRUNO.

in his thought. As soon as one evil is disposed of, another appears; and the more man resists evil, the stronger and more tenacious it becomes.

Jesus said, "Resist not evil" Stop fearing the thing that is troubling you. Stop giving it power in your thought. Stop making something out of nothing. Stop accepting evil as a fact. What you fear and resist will embody itself in your experience according to the proportion or intensity of your resistance. *Resist not evil* means to stop reacting to it in your thought; it means to keep your conditions, problems, symptoms, and physical organs out of your personal mind. If all disease, disorder, and disintegration are in the carnal mind, what you keep out of that mind cannot affect you adversely. St. Paul said, "Be not overcome of evil, but overcome evil with good." To render evil impotent by recognizing nothing but good is the only way out. The evil that comes through the carnal mind can be obliterated only by changing the mind, by reversing the beliefs which keep it in motion. To get at the root cause of all your negative ills and troubles and to eliminate them, you must have a complete change of consciousness. You must "Let this mind be in you which was also in Christ Jesus."

DO NOT SABOTAGE YOUR TREATMENTS

Many people are like a certain woman who went to church to pray over a problem. She spent thirty minutes telling God about it; then she concluded the prayer with the statement that she was now leaving it entirely in His hands. If she had stopped there, everything might have worked out to her satisfaction, and the prayer might have been answered. But she didn't. On the way out of the church, she met a willing listener and related the whole terrible situation to her. In other words, she sabotaged her prayer by taking it out of God's hands and transferring it to her friend's. Jesus said, "Go and tell no man." The space between the prayer and the answer is one of the most important aspects of the prayer, for it is during this time that the action of the prayer is retarded or accelerated. If the treatment is to succeed, the law must be permitted to act in new ways. IT MUST BE LIVED. The promise, "Before they call, I will answer," must be taken literally. All our thoughts, words, and actions must conform to the new ideal which we have set before God. We must not only change our thought out of the old condition and into the new while we are praying, but we must keep it changed twenty-four hours of the twenty-four.

It is a law of mind that whatever we think upon grows and that whatever we refuse to think upon diminishes. Any recital or re-hashing of the negative aspects of a problem after the treatment has been given is to *un*-think, *un*-pray, or to sabotage the treatment. No matter how carefully we may have prepared and given the treatment, the whole structure can be torn down in five minutes given to self-pity, worry, or complaint. The more we think and talk about our trials, problems, shortages, grievances, sufferings, injustices, and misfortunes, the more we will continue to experience unhappiness. Conversely, the more we think upon and praise the blessings we have, the more blessings will come to us. The true way to keep our treatment intact until it has accomplished its purpose is to guide, guard, and discipline our words. "They that dwell in the secret place of the most High [are positive] shall abide under the shadow of the Almighty."

Our affirmations and treatments will be effective only if we realize the Truth back of them and continue in It. They will work for us only if we put feeling and meaning into them and dwell steadfastly upon the desire in completion. To "pray without ceasing" is to keep the thought changed into the new concept we are seeking to bring forth. Emerson said, "Assume a virtue and you shall have the realization." Isaiah said, "He will keep him in perfect peace whole mind is stayed on thee;" and Jesus said, "Remain within my love." In other words, "Act as though I am and I will be." Let your treatment be a glorious realization of the presence of Gcod rather than a striving against evil.

TREAT YOUR TREATMENT

When a treatment backfires (returns to our thought as imperfect or incomplete), or we find our thought going back to it, to the person for whom it was given, or to the outward aspects of the condition we are trying to change, we may be sure that one of two things has happened. We may not yet realize our place in the work of healing, or something in the subjective consciousness may be denying or objective statement.

It is wise at such times to find the reasons for the adulteration and to treat them specifically. There should be no doubt in the mind of the healer as to his place in the treatment. He merely happens to be the one through whom the movement of God's Mind is channeled in this particular case. He has not personal responsibility beyond using his knowledge of the oneness of God and man and exercising his conviction that thought is creative. "I can of mine own self do nothing." . . . . . "It is the Father within that doeth the works," said Jesus, and so must say any one who gives a treatment.

Is there some hostility in the subconscious mind? Then treat the hostility *per se*, knowing that it has no law to support it. Is there doubt? Treat it, knowing that in God it has no basis for existence. Is it the bugaboo of the "difficult" or "incurable?" Treat the false sense of material sight. Is it the appearance of the disease form? Recognize the form for what it is — the outpicturing of a distorted thought, the truth of which is unmarred perfection — perfection which is waiting to be called forth by and through your word. No matter what the appearance or its effect on us, we must change our thought until we see nothing but the quickening, beneficent, harmonious action of the Spirit within the one for whom the treatment is given. We must treat our treatment until our unbelief has been healed, or until we have the full mental acceptance of the word we have released.

This does not mean that we have to repeat the treatment; we must treat the one that has already been given. We do this by declaring that the statement made in treatment is a law unto the person for whom it was given and that it is going to be operative for him. Reverse every contrary, negative, and un-Godlike thought. Declare that the treatment is in harmony with Divine Law, with God and with all Good, and that is it competent to bring about the perfect healing of every circumstance and condition in the patient's life. Know that since it is now a part of God, it cannot fail.

CHAPTER 8

HOW TO TREAT YOURSELF

If all treatment is self-treatment and if the only one to be convinced is the one making the statements, the only difference between treating one's self and treating another person is the direction in which the treatment is pointed. Instead of addressing others, we now address ourselves, and we talk to ourselves until we are convinced of the truth of what we say. What is this self with whom we talk? It is the great subconscious mind that connects us with God and with all supply. It is the larger part of every man—the guarantee of freedom, and of power, and of fulfillment of every right desire. In fact, there is nothing that it cannot do and nothing that it cannot accomplish when the necessary condition has been fulfilled. What is this condition? To trust the Law to complete itself—that is, to shift all responsibility to It. Jesus said, "The things I do, I do not of myself; the Father within, He doeth the works." Just as the momentum of a snowball is determined by size that it attains, the effectiveness of our world is determined by the measure of our trust.

If we impress our treatment upon the subconscious mind with sufficient intensity, faith, and vigor, if we register our claims with sufficient emphasis and trust, and if we do our utmost to actualize our claims, there is nothing in the world that can oppose them or stand in the way of their success. The treatment will gather to itself everything necessary to complete itself. Limp, half-hearted thinking, on the other hand, means limp execution; little or no change occurs in the conditions we are seeking to correct when there is only a slight impression made upon the Creative Mind. The force of registration must not be construed as personal effort or will power; it is a concomitant of the absolute conviction that it is God who is doing the work.

Self-treatment is nothing more than telling the subconscious mind what we want done. Turn your thought inward; relaxing from head to foot, imagine that you see your other self standing before you. Call him by your name and talk to him something after this fashion:

> "Harry (or whatever your name is), you are going to listen to, act upon, and embody every word I speak. Here are my directions: Tonight while I am asleep, I want you to quicken my realization that God, the Good, is the only power operating in my life. Let this idea fill my consciousness so completely that it animates everything in my experience. Let every good I have ever known be increased. Help me to see only the Good, expect only the good, accept only the good, express only the Good. And as I go forth to meet my Good, may I go forth to share my Good."

ANALYSIS OF SELF-TREATMENT

The thing that makes self-treatment effective is the spirit or power that you put into it. In talking yourself out of evil or into good, you must speak your word with authority — that is, speak as one who knows and knows that he knows. You must be so convinced that your word has power, as you release it into the creative activity of the subconscious mind, that there is no suggestion of doubt or compromise in your thought. You do not have to put mental or physical force into your word, but you must be sure of yourself and sure of what you are doing You must have faith in your authority; you must speak your word (give your treatment) with the quiet conviction that it will accomplish that whereunto it is sent and will return from its operation in the great subconscious mind laden with good.

But the first step in self-treatment is the preparation or conditioning of the subconscious mind to receive and to retain the idea projected into it. This is necessary in order that the conscious and subconscious minds can move in the same direction, toward the same end. If the inner mind denies what the outer mind decrees (affirms), the unity of action is destroyed. It is imperative, therefore, that every contradictory and false belief be analyzed and talked out of the mentality before the treatment is given. If we neglect this step, we are trying to walk in two directions at the same time.

The reason you can talk your inner self out of unwanted things is that your subconscious mind reasons deductively. It has no other purpose than to obey your word. It acts by reacting; it responds by corresponding. When this mind has been cleansed of conflicting thoughts, you have absolute dominion over it. It cannot talk back nor choose a line of thinking contrary to your own. It cannot deny or refuse what you ask. What the intellect decrees, the subconscious must obey.

What will you do then when you find a contradiction or denial neutralizing your conscious thought? Continue treating (praying through your mind) until your conscious thought believes and your subconscious mind no longer denies; that is, until the conscious and subconscious minds are unified or integrated. If you are going to objectify a desirable experience, you must have both a conscious and a subconscious realization of that experience in the mind. The action and reaction to your word must be balanced. Since it is the subconscious state of your thought that reacts, the conscious mind must be trained to choose wisely what the Creative Power is to respond to.

TWO METHODS OF SELF-TREATMENT

In talking yourself out of the things you wish to expel from your experience, you should use your formulas not less than three times a day — in the morning before breakfast, at noon before lunch, and at night before you retire. You must be positive in your declarations; you must believe every word that you speak; and you must have absolute faith in your ability to live up to the claims you are making.

Often we address the outer self with the conscious mind and put things right up to ourselves — as an adult might talk to a child, an employer to an employee, or one comrade to another, depending on our individual type and on the situation. This is merely surface treatment; it is all right as far as it goes, but it doesn't go far enough. Here is an example:

"Now, John Doe, (calling yourself by name)," or "Now, young man, there is something wrong with you and you know it. .You are failing because you are only partly alive. You have lost track of your divinity and the good things of life are passing you by. The trouble with you is that you are not demanding enough of yourself. Your resolutions are weak, and your expectations are small. You must do something about this right away. You must think and live to some purpose. You must bring out the best in yourself and put it to work."

If you will study this method, you will see that the thing that is lacking here is spiritual therapy and power. Jesus said, "The natural man receiveth not the things of God." The conscious mind unaided by the subconscious is helpless to execute its commands. In the more powerful form of treatment, you think deeply and penetratively into the subconscious mind; then you say something like this:

> "Subconscious Mind of Me, I need your help right now. I know that you can and will give it to me. Right this minute you are working for me. Make me conscious of God's Presence as the great accomplishing power in my life. Give me both the qualities to triumph over the difficulties in my path and the power to develop those equalities. Make me master over myself and over every situation in my experience. Keep me in touch with God-POWER so that nothing but good can get into my life."

ANOTHER EXAMPLE OF SELF-TREATMENT

"Letting God speak through you is the highest form of prayer."

The right way to get what you want from the Universe is to get it through yourself. Have you ever put your claims right up to your subconscious self and talked to it just as you would talk to a partner or an assistant from whom you expected immediate action?

When you are confronted with an insoluble problem, just address your subconscious self and say:

"Subconscious Mind of Me, I am calling on you in this situation because I know that you are in touch with all wisdom, understanding, and power. I know too that your one and only desire is to help me in my needs. You know what this problem is, and you know that there is a perfect solution to it. You have access to all the intelligence there is; that is why I am commanding you to register the correct solution in and through me now. It is imperative and urgent that I have this information at once; that is why I am calling on you. I know that you cannot fail."

Then set your treatment in motion in some such words as these:

"The solution to this problem is now known in Mind, and is now known in my mind. My mind is conscious of this solution and is conscious of its ability to solve this problem. To that Mind in which I have my being, there is no problem since the solution is already known. I await this answer with absolute and unqualified certainty."

In this type of treatment, you must be certain that your claims are spiritual legal — that is, that they are in accord with the Will and Purpose of God. You are dealing with Law and must not ask for things that are unlawful or harmful to yourself or others.

If the commanding type of treatment troubles you or seems sacrilegious, remember that it is authorized in the Scriptures: "Concerning the work of my hand, command ye Me." Do not, then, beg or beseech God for what you already have, but recognize, affirm, and claim it. Make your claim so strong and press it so hard that there cannot be any doubt as to the nature of the response. "Command ye Me." Be bold. Be sure. Be definite. Be deliberate. Be determined. Be persistent. Know what you want, and know that it is according to the Will and Purpose of God. Then claim it as your own.

SINK OR SWIM TREATMENT

"I create new heavens and a new earth; the former shall not be remembered, nor come into mind." Isa. 65:17.

When percussions, fluoroscopes, stethoscopes, X-rays, blood counts, and basal metabolism tests all tell the same story and the doctor says that nothing can be done, Jesus says, "Leave all and follow me." Leave the diagnosis. Forget the prognosis. Drop the calamity. Dismiss the ultimatum. Turn away from the fear, and jump off the deep end of the relative into the Absolute. Your extremity is now God's opportunity. What man could not do for you on the material plane, God will now do for you on the spiritual.

This is a great climax in your life; the way you meet it will determine the outcome of your trouble. With a death sentence hanging over you, you can no longer look to material means for help but must center your whole thought and faith in God. Your vision must now be one-pointed, and your loyalty undivided. It is now sink or swim, die or live. When you come to this place, the whole universe is back of you, working out a miracle in your life. The diseased body will now be absorbed into the power of God, and the old beliefs will now fade away like shadows before the dawn.

But where are you going when you follow Him? You are going from a physical thing called disease into a spiritual thing called perfection. You are going into a new height or dimension of consciousness where "the former [things] shall not be remembered nor come into mind."

DEEP END TREATMENT IN TIME OF DESPAIR*

"I know that all of the Life of the Universe streams through my body at this moment. I know that Mind knows nothing of such things as incurable conditions. I know that the only thing that hinders my complete restoration right now is my own blindness to Truth. From this moment I affirm my oneness with the Divine Perfection. I drop my belief in the actuality of disease, and affirm my faith in the Perfect Presence within. I do not have to call to a far-distant God who sits in the heavens. The God of the Universe is within me now. He has been there all my life, never forcing Himself upon me, but momentarily awaiting my recognition. All my life I have been blind, but now my eyes are open to the truth, and the truth sets me free from the law of sin and death.

"At this moment I dwell upon the fact that this great Creative Law of Mind, awaits my word. I speak my word for the manifestation in me of all that Spirit is in Itself. I give thanks for my uncovered Perfection, and I release myself lock, stock, and barrel, diagnosis, prognosis, and feelings, to the Creative Activity of Mind."

WAYS TO SPEED YOUR RECOVERY

"True religion and medicine," says Dr. J. M. Finnery, "should go hand in hand as complementary forces." *True religion* is the practical application of the principles of Truth; it deepens faith, renews the body, spiritualizes the mind, expands the consciousness, releases power and bears fruit in all good works. It is the Life of God in the soul of man.

Let us keep our mental levels high by removing all the thought barriers to our good and by looking ever unto God, "Who forgiveth all our iniquities, Who healeth all our diseases."

SEVEN WAYS TO SPEED YOUR RECOVERY

1. REMOVE ALL LIMITATIONS by casting from your mind every adverse thought or belief which would oppose your healing. Keep your entire thought centered in Wholeness. Life is God. Know that It cannot be limited or bound in any way.

2. CONTROL YOUR IMAGINATION by refusing to allow it to play upon negative images, appearances, or the careless suggestions of others.

3. SUBLIMATE YOUR FEAR EMOTIONS by identifying yourself with the Love of God. Replace the negative emotions with those so strongly positive that the negative are literally destroyed.

4. KEEP YOURSELF RELAXED by giving up all thoughts of tension and by dwelling upon the peaceful Presence of God. Know that God is powerful enough to cope with any situation in your body. "In quietness and confidence shall be your strength."

5. KEEP YOURSELF RECEPTIVE TO WARD GOD by giving Him all the power in your life and by centering your thought in the Christ Presence which is untouched by sickness, disease, or contagion of any kind.

6. PLACE YOURSELF, YOUR BODY, AND ALL YOUR AFFAIRS LOVINGLY IN GOD'S HANDS. "The Light of God surrounds me; the Love of God enfolds me; the Power of God protects me; the Presence of God watches over me. Wherever I am, God is."

7. TRANSMUTE YOUR PAIN by knowing that your body is pure spiritual substance in every cell and that Spirit is present in the very place where the manifestation of pain is trying to make itself felt.

PRAYER FOR A HOSPITAL

"Heavenly Father, I thank Thee for this house of healing, for it is a sign of Thy tender mercy. Bless the doctors, nurses, and all who serve here, and grant them wisdom, skill, and patience as they wait upon Thy suffering children. Reward them with knowing that their work is holy, for they labor together with Thee. Raise up friends for this place that its work may be maintained by Thy glory through Jesus Christ our Lord. Amen."

CHAPTER 9

HOW TO TREAT OTHERS

"Bear ye one another's burdens, and so fulfill the law of Christ."
GAL. 6:2.

Today's lesson is a plan for spiritual treatment that may be used by anybody, anywhere, at any time, for anyone in need of treatment, no matter who he is, where he is, or what may be wrong with him. In a nut shell, the alpha and omega (the beginning and the end) of every treatment is, as Ernest Holmes says, to "Resolve the whole thing, theoretically, into mind and change the thought about it."

Spiritual treatment involves not only the neutralizing of diseased and distorted thought forms but also the affirmations of something that is not apparent. We must pray not only until our conscious thought accepts and embodies what we specify in the treatment but also until our subconscious thought no longer rejects, contradicts, or denies it. Just as pure water flowing from the faucet into a glass half full of mud will quickly clean out of the mud, spiritual ideas ceaselessly flowing into the consciousness of a diseased and sick body will quickly cleanse and restore the body.

Begin your treatment by getting into a position that will assure perfect and complete mental and physical relaxation. Relaxation may be difficult at first, but it can be induced by quietly contemplating the Presence of God and by realizing that the good you are seeking for another is seeking him through you. Then know, that in spite of the disease which has made its appearance upon his body, there can be no separation between him and God. Declare that anything unlike God has no basis for existence and therefore is unreal. Say:

"This man is Spirit, and Spirit cannot be sick. The same Mind that was in Christ Jesus is in him. It is All-Powerful, Creative, and instant in action. It knows everything, is everything, and does everything. It is now providing ways and means for the fulfillment and perfect outworking of this treatment."

Then call your patient by name and address, and give your treatment, continuing it until you are satisfied that the work has been accomplished.

"John Doe of 7489 Madison Ave., New York City, this word is for you. You are a perfect expression of Divine Life and Power."

EXAMPLE OF TREATMENT FOR ANOTHER

If you were to ask the author what he considers most important in giving a treatment he would reply, "The realization that it is God who is doing the work and not the healer." A good healer never takes personal responsibility for the outcome of any treatment any more than he takes credit for the good that is accomplished. Knowing that the movement and action of the Universal Mind are purely mechanical, he realizes that his only responsibility is to set the Law in motion. This realization frees him from all anxiety, nervousness, and doubt.

Next in importance for the healer is the realization that he is not attempting to heal disease, circumstances, or conditions but is working solely with the consciousness of the sufferer.

The treatment for healing has no relation whatsoever to the thing being treated, for there can be no relationship between health and sickness. If disease were real, it would be like God, Truth, or Love, and nothing in the universe could change it. It is because it is unreal that it can be healed. The treatment is a living declaration of the Truth that restores the consciousness of Wholeness in the patient. The healing takes place when all doubts and false pictures have been dissolved and when harmony has been restored. It is manifest when the healer sees the patient as perfect.

We begin a treatment for another person by calling his name and address and by saying in effect:

"John Doe, this word is for you. It is the Law which is going to be operative for you. Your life is an expression of the Perfect Life of God. In you there is no disease, sickness or limitation of any kind. There is no overaction, inaction, or false action of any atom, organ, or function of your body. The one radiant Life flows through you, cleanses you, harmonizes you, renews you, heals you, and makes you every whit whole. The Presence of God awakens in you sufficient energy, guidance, wisdom, and understanding to do anything you undertake to do. This Presence of Life rebuilds and restores every part of your body as you relax and let it act. Nothing can express through your physical being that it not perfect. Receive the fulfillment of these claims now. In the Name of the Father, and the Son, and of the Holy Ghost. Amen."

The reason the metaphysical treats himself to know the truth about his patient or treats himself for what the patient thinks is wrong with him is found in Jesus' words: "First, cast out the beam out of thine own eye; then thou shalt see clearly to cast the mote out of thy brother's eye." The word also explains why the consciousness of the practitioner affects the consciousness of the patient. If the practitioner with the intention of healing his patient acts within himself to neutralize, reverse, and drive out of his consciousness all negative thoughts, the patient to whom he directs the treatment will receive the healing. Why? Because the patient is his own concept. He and the patient are in the same Mind, and what is known in one part of Mind is known in all parts equally and at the same time. The truth that the practitioner establishes in his own mind about the patient will arise in the consciousness of the patient automatically.

TREATMENT FOR CHILDREN

Children are particularly responsive to metaphysical treatment because of their faith, confidence, and obedience to authority. The child does not make up his mind that he cannot get well or that one disease is harder to heal than another; consequently, he has little resistance to spiritual help. Since there are few inhibitions or conflicts in his mind, the receptivity essential for spiritual healing is already there. The thing that is likely to inhibit or delay the healing of a child is the parent's doubt or fear. In situations in which the parent's emotions are deeply involved, it is wise to secure the services of a metaphysical healer to treat the child impersonally and without fear. Why? Because any doubt, uncertainty, worry, or fear tends to be incorporated in the treatment and nullifies any healing activity.

We are really capable of thinking about only one thing at a time. Naturally, the strongest thought has the right of way.

Since we tend to act upon that to which we give our attention, this thought will eventually express itself in action. To assist a child in overcoming weakness of any sort, the adult has only to plant in the subconscious mind the seed he wishes to come to fruition.

The best time to treat a child is just before he goes to sleep at night. When the child is relaxed and entering sleep, his subconscious mind is most receptive and responsive to the invigorating thoughts of truth. Simply sit by his bed, holding his hand gently in your and say:

"Johnny, you are now listening to every word I say to you. Your sleep is going to be restful, healing, and renewing. The Power of God is now active in you. It flows freely through your body, cleansing, healing, vitalizing, harmonizing, adjusting, and restoring every part. You are one with this Life and Power; in It you are made every whit whole. You will awaken tomorrow morning a new boy in Christ — strong, perfect, and whole."

In order to help a child for whom school is difficult, you may say:

> "Johnny, you are going to enter into your kingdom. There is no barrier to your learning. You share with your classmates all the Intelligence, Wisdom, and Understanding there is. God in you appears in the classroom as curiosity, interest, reason, judgment, memory, pride in achievement, power to cooperate, and sense of well-being. Your learning will be meaningful, and your growth a joyous and happy process."

SYMPATHETIC SUFFERING

"A merry heart doeth good like a medicine: but a broken spirit drieth the bones." PR. 17:22.

Those who are impelled to suffer with the sick should ask themselves these questions: "Have I done everything in my power to relieve and help the one who is sick? Have I done all I can to make him comfortable and happy? Have I done my utmost to help him recover? Do I improve his condition by being miserable with him? Do I help him by grieving and being unhappy over his illness? Do I improve his attitude by fear and worry?" If your answer to the first three questions is *Yes*, your answer to the last three is obviously *No*.

We should remind ourselves in situation of this kind that it is convention that decrees sympathetic suffering between the healthy and the sick, and not God. Morbid, sorrowful, depressed state of mind in those associated with sick persons have a tendency to further depress them. All doctors and metaphysicians stress the importance of cheerfulness and mental sunshine in the cure of sickness. Fear and anxiety cast gloom around the patient and retard his recovery. Genuine cheerfulness, on the other hand, is stimulating, soothing, and healing. A mock cheerfulness (which is nothing more than a cover for grief) is even more devastating and depressing to the sick than sadness. It is about as beneficial and effective as the grin on the face of a skeleton.

When the writer of Proverbs said that "A merry heart doeth good like a medicine," he was stressing the therapeutic value of a happy emotional climate. The greatest contribution we can make to the sick is to be genuinely happy in their presence. If we have met the requirements of the first three questions in this lesson, we can feel content that we have done all that we are capable of doing. Cheerfulness is to the mind and body what sunshine is to the plants and trees. It not only brings out the best in the mind but gives food, life, energy, and power of recovery to the body.

FEAR FOR LOVES ONES

Many students have told the author that they can do wonderful things through the power of prayer, but that when it comes to the needs of loved ones or members of their immediate families, they are utterly helpless. When one realizes that the first requirement of spiritual healing is to be able to impersonalize not only the condition from which the patient may be suffering but also the patient himself, this difficulty is not hard to understand. It is comparatively easy to impersonalize people for whom we have no strong feeling, but when it comes to those near and dear to us, we are likely to become frantic, frightened, and depressed. We call the doctor and can hardly wait until he comes. We rush to the drug store to get the medicines he prescribes. We pray in every way we know and do everything we can. We pace the floor and refuse food and sleep. We pray, beg, beseech, implore, affirm, declare, and hope. Then, weakened and torn by fear and uncertainty, we sit down in bewilderment and await the worst.

If you have never kept a vigil of this kind, you cannot appreciate the mental anguish and suffering of those who have. The greatest barrier to recovery in a very sick person, however, is the apprehension of his friends and of those close to him. If there ever is a time when ne needs to be calm, peaceful, and collected, it is during serious illness. We would not think of pumping carbon monoxide or other lethal toxins into a sick room; but we let ourselves be fearful, and fear poisons the very atmosphere that the sick one breathes.

The proper thing to do at such a time is to put ourselves in tune with God. We should do everything on the material plane that we can, but primarily we must establish peace and harmony within our own minds. Instead of giving way to fear and worry, we should remind ourselves that we are not dealing with persons, conditions, and things but only with our thought concerning persons, conditions, and things. We should sit down in the silence and treat ourselves for peace, and for faith and confidence about the one who is sick. The spiritual uplift of the healer will benefit the patient in two ways: it will accelerate the healing (it may even bring about complete recovery if the consciousness of perfection is strong enough), and it will remove fear from the atmosphere. When fear is removed, the work for the sick one becomes easy.

DO NOT GIVE IN OR GIVE UP

The fear of death is so strong in most people that it impedes their health, lessens their span of life, and affects their business and income adversely. In fact, there is no limitation that is not in the last analysis directly traceable to man's fear of death. It will be profitable to us to analyze this fear and to face the imposter at once. What is the fear belief about death? It is a belief in a power *over* us instead of a power *within* us. How did the belief come? Jesus said *by man*. How is it to be overcome? Again Jesus said *by man*. In other words, man conceived the idea of death and man is the one to meet or rise above it in his own consciousness by changing his mental attitude toward it (making it of no importance in his mind), and by giving the full power of his thought to Life.

If premature death is a matter of giving up, thousands of people could be saved every year by the determination to live. We have known many cases where Life triumphed over death because someone refused to let the mind act with the belief in death. If the mind and will are so completely identified with Life that the power of life is increased, the patient will live. If they are given over to death, he will die. But, in either event, the result is always a matter of belief and the attitude of the patient. Yes, one may touch bottom and return again to the top by increasing the power of life in his own mind. When we rationalize the belief about death, we shall have less sickness, grief, and poverty. We shall be freed from more fear than the fear of death.

It is important in the crisis of serious illness, however, not to allow a person to die until every measure for prolonging his life has been exhausted. The practice of refusing to give in to death will produce greater results than any other. Why? Because the subconscious mind always acts with the strongest emotion and always magnifies and increases whatever it is given to act upon. When the conscious mind is quiescent or out of focus as in the case of impending death, the forces of death are sure to win. The process can be changed, however, by a change of identity and a reversal of one's faith. Identify yourself with death, and the subconscious mind increases the power of death. Identify yourself with Life, and the subconscious mind increases the power of your life.

Robert A. Russell

CHAPTER 10

B C N

"Back in the days of sail, these three signal flags, B C N, meant, 'I will not abandon you.' The lookout spies a ship-wrecked seaman tossing in an open boat. To give the poor fellow courage and assurance while he is shortening sail and wearing his ship about, the captain breaks out this signal: 'Hold on! I will not abandon you.'

"Are you in distress? Sick? Anxious? Afraid? In any kind of trouble? God's signal is flying: 'Courage! Trust me. I will never leave you nor forsake you.'

"Pain is a mystery. Often pain is our enemy. It drains away our resistance. It strikes us down to become victims of other evils. Very well, then, fight pain as your enemy. Your doctor fights for you as He guards you against more pain. Your nurse fights for you as she smooths your bed and gives you some of her courage along with the ice bag. Christ fights for you. He knows what pain is. You shan't have more than you can bear.

"But pain is also your friend. It is a red signal of danger ahead. We escape death a thousand times because God has given us pain. Pain alone can show us that grand side of life of which ease knows nothing. Pain is the furnace and the hammering that make us tough and resilient as coiled springs, patient, brave, mindful of others. Pain can lead us to God. 'An enemy? Fight him. A friend? Use him!'"*

---

* *THE FORWARD MOVEMENT, Sharon, Pennsylvania.*

"HE SHALL SUSTAIN THEE."

Eternal Father, strong to save, stretch forth Thy hand and heal me, Thy servant. I put my trust in Thee. Grant me such a sense of Thy indwelling Presence that I may commit myself wholly to Thy care. Thy love enfolds me. Thy strength will sustain me. Grant me patience in my suffering. Draw me nearer to my Savior, the Divine Sufferer. Conform me more and more to His Likeness. In His present companionship, may I find peace and quiet. Thus conquering pain, purified in life, and restored to health and strength, may I be more meet for Thy service through Jesus Christ our Lord. Amen.

HEART TROUBLE

"Let not your heart be troubled." JOHN 14:27

Heart trouble, according to specialists, government reports, and insurance companies is America's *Number One Killer*. Yet to the victims of this uncertain and dread disease, Jesus Christ offers certainty, correction, coordination, renewing, healing, and wholeness. The the materially minded, this mighty, redeeming, adjusting Power of God will sound like no remedy at all, and many will pass it by as pure imagination. But when the facts are known and understood, its virtue and power are quickly apparent.

Let us inquire first into some of the many factors which produce heart trouble. They are legion, of course, but the chief one, according to the best doctors, is the mental and physical tension of modern living. The persons most addicted to heart trouble are the burden bearers, the responsibility carriers, the worried, the fearful, the impatient, the sensitive, the nervous; those whose minds are rightly orientated toward God seldom suffer from so-called heart trouble. We must, as Jesus pointed out, look to the mind, attitudes, as emotions for the cause of this serious ailment.

When Jesus said to His disciples, "Let not your heart be troubled, neither let it be afraid," He was speaking to the mind and emotional nature of man. He was saying, "Be not fearful, worried, troubled, anxious, nor apprehensive. Let no anger, hate, revenge, nor condemnation govern you. Let no inharmony, depression, doubt, nor bitterness radiate from your heart. Release your disturbing belief in the power of evil. Do not despair. Let go of the burdens which weigh so heavily upon you. Let not your MIND be troubles, either." "That sounds reasonable," you say, "but how can I do it? How can I reestablish the rhythm, harmony, peace, and poise that will keep my heart sound and strong?" You can do it through feeling after God and by realizing that in your heart is centered the Love of God which can be likened to an every-flowing stream, bearing abundant blessing to you in its course and carrying onward to others the blessing of the peace and joy which you have made your own.

> MY HEART IS CONTROLLED BY DIVINE PEACE AND CALM. IT IS UNTROUBLED, FEARLESS, AND STRONG. ITS ACTION IS HARMONIOUS AND TRUE.

AN OUNCE OF PREVENTION

"Take no thought for your life, what ye shall eat, or what ye shall drink; nor yet for your body, what ye shall put on. Is not the life more than meat, and the body than raiment?" — MATT. 6:25.

Taking no thought for your life does not mean living in a thoughtless state of existence, but rather taking away the anxiety and the sense of responsibility which we tend to attach to things. If taking thought about things creates wear and tear, friction, and tension, taking no thought will result in harmony and peace.

PREVENTIVES AND ANTIDOTES FOR HEART CONDITIONS

1. Give up all the injurious habits that react directly upon the heart with bad effect, such as smoking, drinking, over-eating, late hours, and excesses of all kinds.

2. Avoid the sense of hurry. Do not allow obligations and the weight of responsibilities to pile up in your mind. Think only one thing at a time.

3. Never allow yourself to be driven by outside pressure; never think of any problem as impossible of solution. Avoid all sense of conflict between duty and desire, and all sense of defeat, frustration, and self pity.

4. Never feel that you are not needed or that you are pushed aside, by-passed, superceded, or out-of-date. Never admit any thought of fear, worry, inferiority, or repression; and never try to defend yourself for anything you say or do.

5. If your heart has been acting up, deliberately develop the expectation of recovery. Stop being serious, fearful, or worried; develop a sense of humor if you do not have it. Learn to laugh at yourself and at others. Build up a sense of detachment, self-confidence, and self-esteem. Face very problem objectively and impersonalize it

when it comes. View it from afar, and side-step it, by handing it over to God and leaving it in His Hands.

6. Acquire an inward consciousness of peace; maintain it at all times and under all circumstances. Move slowly, Eat slowly. Decide slowly and react slowly. Take at least fifteen minutes to get out of bed in the morning and never run to the telephone, door, street car, or bus. Refuse to become excited or emotional over anything. Take your time about everything. You have all eternity before you.

THE PATIENCE OF CHRIST NOW EXPRESSED IN ME HAS REMOVED ALL IMPATIENCE FROM MY HEART.

NERVES

The people who suffer from fidgets, hysteria, palpitation, tension, agitation, indecision, irregular heart action, emotional outbreaks, and other so-called nervous disorders are not suffering from nerves at all but from thoughts and states of mind which interfere with the natural rhythm of the body. The trouble is not in the nerves but in the thought and feeling stimulating them. The nerves are simply tough white cords of tissue that connect the cells of the brain with the cells of the body. They serve much as telephone wires do, except that each is a one-way transmitter. Some nerves bring messages to the brain and spinal cord; other carry orders from this central control to the muscles of the body. One cannot impute symptoms to diseased nerves, for the nervous system is purely a mechanism.

The difficulty is in the mind that presides over this wonderful system and employs it to control the body. If the prevailing states of mind are negative, agitated, fearful, worried, hateful, troubled, intolerant, antagonistic, critical, or condemnatory, the result will be irritation, tension, confusion, and disorder in the nerves.

The real cure for jaded nerves is not in medicine, sedatives, or the communicating apparatus but in controlled, orderly, and disciplined thinking. To have peace, health, and perfection in the nerves, we must have peace, health, and perfection in the mind. God is peace; to claim His peace and to open the mind to it will free the nerves from all tension and disorder. Robert Louis Stevenson said, "Quiet minds cannot be perplexed or frightened but go on in fortune or misfortune at their own private pace like the ticking of a clock during a thunderstorm."

Here then are the two steps to take in curing nervous troubles:

1. Mentally detach yourself from all irritating things.

2. Fill yourself so completely with the peace of God that it radiates to everybody and everything.

I AM AN ACTIVE CHANNEL FOR THE INFLOW AND OUTFLOW OF DIVINE PEACE. IT FILLS ME TO SUCH AN EXTENT THAT IT RULES EVERY- THING IN MY LIFE. CENTERED IN THE PEACE OF GOD, I AM UNDISTURBED BY ANYTHING THAT HAPPENS IN MY WORLD.

ALCOHOL ADDICTION

"Put ye on the Lord Jesus Christ and make not provision for the flesh, to fulfill the lusts thereof." ROMANS 13:14

That there is no permanent help or cure for chronic alcoholism outside of mental and spiritual therapeutics has been shown times without number. Like any other injurious habit, it is the product of a mental state and not merely a physical manifestation. Let us consider the true nature of this affliction to see how it can be met.

The reason most of the known methods of meeting this problem (medicine, scolding, condemnation, institutes, and jail) have failed is that they attack the problem at the wrong end. This is true also of moral suasion. Where the will is weak and the moral tone is low, moral suasion can have little effect. Many liquor addicts turn to a psychiatrist for help, but here again is the danger of overlooking the soul behind the mind of the patient. The metaphysician, on the other hand, combines both the human and the divine elements in his therapy.

When one understands that the real source of the trouble in this affliction is in the subconscious mind and in the habit patterns of the victim, he attacks the problem at this point. It makes no difference whether the habit was initiated by grief, worry, or misfortune, or in the search for some new thrill or sensation, there is always a great weakness and lack of self control at the seat of the trouble.

It has been found by most metaphysicians that the best time for treating the unhappy victim of this habit is in the Silence of the Spirit while he is asleep. Very simply and firmly, awaken him to a realization of his true self through your positive declarations. Declare that he does not love liquor but that he loves God. Declare his freedom from the hypnotism of sense stimulation. Declare that God is the only control and power in his life. Declare that Christ has made him free from all weakness, bondage, and false appetites. Affirm strength and freedom for him; then see him strong and free. Drop all anxiety from your mind; know that the Father within does the work and that He never fails. Then use this treatment and keep using it in deep faith and conviction until the confidence and balance of the victim have been restored:

> God is the only power in your life. No adverse habit can have dominion over you, the perfect son of God. Christ gives you freedom from all bondage, and strength to meet every need. You have perfect control over yourself, and you do not give in to any false appetite. Awake, Sleeper, and assume your sonship.

"IMAGINITIS"

Imaginitis is one of the worst diseases on record. It contaminates, shatters, terrifies, perverts, devastates, blights, corrupts, and damns. It makes life a hell for its victims. It creates sickness, divides the mind, distorts the soul, and destroys the body. It makes you think you are sick when you aren't. It makes you think you have something when you haven't. It makes a mountain out of a molehill. It sees the worst in everything, expects the worst, and plans for the worst. It cripples the forces of the system, darkens the consciousness, and creates cowards. The doctor may call it an "oversensitive nature," but the metaphysician labels it "imaginitis."

The word may be new to you, but the symptoms are common to us all. For some unknown reason, we imagine that we are ill. We develop all the aches and pains common to the thing we think is wrong. We are like the man who, after reading a medical book, imagined that he had every disease mentioned in the book except "housemaid's knee." Dr. W. L. Sadler says in a recent issue of *Sharing*, "Thousands of suffering souls are held today by the chain of imaginary bondage. They have no real physical disease. Their ailment is in reality only a 'spiritual infirmity!' They might go free at any time, but they do not know it; they will not believe it. These prisoners of despair are held securely in their prison house of doubt by the force of fear and habit."

How shall we control this factor of imagination and make it do our bidding? We must purify the imagination and keep its reactions true. "Create in me a clean heart and renew a right Spirit within me." This is the work of the Holy Spirit in the soul—to cleanse, renew, and restore. We must render symptoms and trouble harmless by meeting them with a calm, peaceful, and self-possessed attitude of mind. Then we must keep preoccupied with the Good—keep the mind filled with thought of God. . . . "Whatsoever things are true, whatsoever things are honest, whatsoever things are just, whatsoever things are pure, whatsoever things are lovely, whatsoever things are of good report . . . think on these things." We must, too, protect our thought at the source. "If . . . thine eye be single, thy whole body shall be full of light." Apply these principles diligently and steadfastly every day, and your *imaginitis* will disappear.

CHAPTER 11

SHALL I GO TO A DOCTOR?

The question is not whether you shall or shall not go to a doctor, but whether you need a doctor and whether you have faith in him. When we understand that there is one Principle of healing (*vis medicatrix naturae*) inherent in all living things, and that all methods of healing employ and cooperate with the One, we shall see doctors, nurses, hospitals, medicines, and external appliances as spiritual ideas through which God works. The really vital and important thing after all is not the method or means employed in healing but the patient's degree of faith or acceptance. Jesus said, "Thy faith hath made thee whole." Destroy this faith, and you kill the virtue of the method. Faith in medicine and faith in God produce the same result. If God is omnipresent, He is in one place as much as in another. He must be, then, as present in a pill or plaster as He is in a spiritual treatment.

Then, why use medicine at all? Why not rely upon spiritual means altogether and abolish all others?

Individuals live on different levels of mental acceptance, just as they did in the days of the healing miracles of Jesus. Even a cursory reading of the Biblical records of healing will show that He always suited His therapy and teaching to the plane upon which He found the person in need. Some persons were healed at a great distance by His spoken word; others were healed by the laying on of hands. One woman was healed by touching the hem of His garment. In the case of the blind man, Jesus annointed his eyes with clay. Why clay? Was there any magic or virtue in the clay? No! He used it because He knew the need of the blind man for some material sign upon which he could pin his faith.

Let us be sensible about our religion; let us keep our feet on the ground. If our consciousness is not high enough at the moment to demonstrate over our physical ills, let us call a doctor. Let us use both the spiritual and the material. If we need the crutches of material action and of other therapies, let us use them and bless them until we no longer need them. If there is but one Healing Principle in the universe and if God is All, medicine and metaphysics are two ends of the same thing. They but two paths to the same goal. Faith operates through both, and God heals through both.

THE DOCTOR CANNOT HEAL YOU BY HIMSELF

Why is it that one person does better under hospital treatment than another? Why is it that one accelerates his healing and another retards it? The answers to these questions are found in the attitude and prevailing state of mind of the patient. He may be positive or negative, responsive or unresponsive. If he is inclined to resist mentally the things that are being done for him, he will set up a state of tension and confusion in his body. If he is unfriendly toward his environment and toward the methods of therapy being administered, he will delay his healing.

It is imperative, therefore, that one not only control his reactions to the external forces about him but also that he keep his thinking true. There is a right way and a wrong way to do everything; the right way to cooperate in a hospital is to maintain a calm, loving, receptive and happy spirit and to agree with and to bless everything that is being done. This acceptance and approval are the patient's part in the healing process; to ignore the responsibility handicaps the doctor and nurses and prolongs the illness. To get quick and good results in medical as well as in metaphysical therapy, the treatment must be a cooperative enterprise between patient and doctor.

Why do we lay so much stress upon the patient's part in the healing process? Because all healing in eh final analysis is self-healing. Dr. Titus Bull, the great neurologist, says, "Matter is spirit at a lower rate of vibration. When a patient is cured, it is the spirit in the cell doing the healing according to its own inherent pattern. No doctor ever yet cured a patient. All he can do is to make it possible for the patient to heal himself." We stress prayer and the practice of Truth in every mode of healing to condition and equalize the body forces. When the body forces are balanced, the healing Principle works with greater precision, momentum, satisfaction, and effect. When the old chronic, putrefying, and adverse thought barriers have been removed, the Spirit rises in us and heals us. The Word becomes flesh.

RIDING TWO HORSES AT THE SAME TIME

Before one can successfully employ the metaphysical Principle in healing, he must first have faith in a power above and beyond himself. To the metaphysician, faith is just as impersonal and automatic as the Principle of Life itself. It acts only on those things that the individual believes to be real. "If a man believes that God is real and that disease is real, He has a divided faith, and the faith that he has in God is negatived by the faith that he has in disease. Therefore, metaphysics must be called in to solve the problem. If we cannot on the physical plane have a faith in God which is not negatived by the contrary faith we have in something else, then we must somehow learn to get behind the outward appearances of things and think upon a plane where the disease (or other form of evil) does not as a matter of fact exist."*

What does one find when he goes behind the "outward appearances of things?" Just what the physicist finds when he resolves matter back into its basic elements; he learns that the real world is spiritual and that it is wholly good. Please do not misunderstand this point. The true metaphysician does not say that there is no evil on the relative plane; he knows that everything on that plane is just as real as it is supposed to be; but he does say that evil must not be recognized or empowered with faith. He believes with St. Paul that faith must be directed to God only. The metaphysician overcomes evil by the principle of non-resistance, or non-recognition. He refuses to give power to evil in his thought or action; he looks through the evil to God.

The reason we have gotten such poor results in practice is that we have been trying to ride two horses at the same time. We have been trying to follow two ideas and get one result. We have tried to be in the darkness and in the light at the same moment. The metaphysician knows this to be an utter impossibility and so seeks to inculcate within each individual an understanding of the universe that is compatible with faith. When this understanding has been reached, everything else will take care of itself. Everything will fall into its right place.

---

* *Quoted from Elbert B. Holmes in THE HEALING EVANGEL by Dr. A. J. Gayner Banks.*

TWO HEADS ARE SOMETIMES BETTER THAN ONE

The old saying that two heads are better than one refers to the combined power of two minds. Often when we become involved in sickness, conflict, or disagreement, we must have outside help in order to restore harmony. It makes no difference whether we call the person who aids us practitioner, healer, or friend; his one and only function at such a time is to help us get a clear conviction, or inner realization of the Truth that is to make us free. He unites his clearer consciousness with ours in the objective we are seeking to demonstrate and continues to the point of touching it. Then as we hold the objective in consciousness, it manifests itself in experience.

Jesus expressed this same law when He said: "If two of you agree on earth as touching anything they shall ask, it shall be done for them of my Father which is in heaven." "If, then, one man has a certain power of mind, two men would have twice as much; and if either or both could call upon Spirit in its Universal mode to contribute toward securing a specific design, the aggregate would be limited only by the imagination of the men. It is like the two poles of a magnet. When Professor Henry of Princeton experimented with the lifting power of a magnet, he suspended a large magnet from a rafter and lifted a few pounds of iron. He then wrapped the magnet with wire and charged it with the current from a small battery. Instead of only a few pounds, the now highly charged magnet lifted 3,000 pounds. That is what will happen when two or more people agree in mind that they can call upon the Universal Mind to contribute its Power and Intelligence.

"Belle Fourche, South Dakota, needed rain to save the crops and fill the reservoirs. L. A. Gleyre, publisher of the Northwest

Post, advertised for it. He ran an ad in his paper asking for two or more inches of rain by the following Wednesday midnight. Imagine the interest he aroused. Everybody wanted rain, but all had mentally speculated on not getting it. Now they all joined in hoping that the ad would prove effective. They changed their thinking of the drouth and its effects to thoughts of rain and its benefits. It is now history that six hours after midnight on Thursday following the indicated Wednesday, it rained two inches or more."

CHAPTER 12

THE TRIPARTITE NATURE OF MAN

"I pray God your whole spirit and soul and body be preserved blameless." THESS. 5:23.

THE BODY: Man is built upon three planes. At the lower part of his being and connecting him with the visible universe is the flesh made of the "dust of the ground," subject to the material laws of a material universe. Here the downward pull on the soul takes place. Here arise the strongest temptations. "They that are after the flesh do mind the things of the flesh," says St. Paul, and then he concludes that "To be carnally minded is death." This would be a hopeless state for man if he did not possess the power of choice and if his whole nature were wholly physical.

THE SOUL: Above, around, supporting, and penetrating the fleshly body (and discovered only by reflection) is the organizing and building principle of man's being, the soul; it unites him with both the lower and higher creation. The human body is maintained not alone by voluntary (conscious) effort, but by involuntary (subconscious) activity; the greater of these is the subconscious.

Dr. A. J. Gayner Banks says, "We are conscious of instincts and appetites, and act upon them, and so far as our natural consciousness is concerned, that is the end. We feel hungry and we eat; we feel angry and we act accordingly; but the action of which we are conscious is only a part of the whole.

"Our soul, without orders, carries on various intricate processes, and so, despite our ignorance, our physical life is maintained, and the necessary adjustments made."

THE SPIRIT: At the top of man's being, he is spirit. Spirit is the part of him that reaches out from the relative (material world) to the Absolute (spiritual world) and distinguishes him from the animal. Through his spirit, man unites himself with the knowledge, substance, wisdom, and power of God.

Now reading from the bottom up, we see that man's unity depends upon the interaction and harmonious working of all three parts, and that no part can be perfect or imperfect without involving the perfection or imperfection of the other two. "The Mind of the Spirit is life and peace."

THERE IS NO REALITY APART FROM SPIRIT

It is obvious that man is conscious on three planes at the same time: sense-consciousness (the body), self-consciousness (the soul), and God-consciousness (Spirit). First in importance is the spiritual (Divine Idea), second the mental, and third the physical.

Just as a ship on the high seas with its sails down and its engines shut off is at the mercy of the storms and deep currents, man living only by the transitory and perishable values of his carnal and intellectual natures is at the mercy of every false belief and destructive element in the race mind. But man is also spirit; consequently, he has the power to master the lower nature and to cause it to work in harmony with the Higher.

Now, let us look at the body. Science tells us that the elements composing the physical body are in a constant state of flux and that they come and go so rapidly (being born and dying) that a man actually does not get up in the morning with the same body he took to bed the night before. In fact, says the scientist, man gets an entirely new body every eleven months. Then why doesn't he express this newness outwardly? Why does he perpetuate the ills of his body from one day to another? Because he does not change his thought of himself despite the change in his body.

Turning now to the soul, we find another swiftly moving stream which is no more permanent than the fluctuating body. Through it flow our thoughts, beliefs, feelings, impulses; it houses our countless selves, and none is more real than the constituent elements of the flesh. One day we are strong, and the next day weak. One day we are brave, and the next day cowardly. And who can discern reality?

There is no reality apart from Spirit. Behind all these transitory selves is another Self that lives forever, birthless, deathless, and imperishable—a self that gives man dominion over all the earth.

THE INNER MAN IS SPIRITUAL; I AM THAT IN-
NER MAN.

CULTIVATING THE MIND OF THE SPIRIT

"The mind of the flesh is death, but the mind of the spirit is life and peace." ROMANS 8:6.

When the metaphysician speaks of the carnal or natural man, he is talking about a man who is only partly awake. His body is awake, and his soul is awake, but his spirit is asleep. In other words, the carnal man is spiritually unaware. Untouched by the Higher forces, his larger self lies dormant within him. In the carnal mind, man lives in the flesh and is controlled by it; in the Christ Mind, he lives above the flesh and triumphs over it.

To those seeking spiritual healing, it is of the utmost importance not only to discipline the mind and its thinking but also to get the correct view and understanding of the body. If the body is to be impregnated with the healing power of Spirit, we must, as St. Paul said, habitually think of it as the temple of the Holy Spirit. "What! Know ye not that your body is the temple of the Holy Ghost, which is in you, which ye have of God; and ye are not your own? For ye are bought with a price: Therefore, glorify God in your body, and in your Spirit, which are God's."

Henry Ward Beecher once said: "God made the human body, and it is by far the most exquisite and wonderful organization which has come to us from the Divine hand. It is a study for one's whole life. If an undevout astronomer is mad, an undevout physiologist is still madder." Jesus had much to say about the body, but He never considered it apart or separate from the Spirit. The body is an outward and visible sign of an inward and spiritual Presence.

"The countenance is a clear index of the spirit that is within, and the body is built up by the soul. Many people think of the soul as if it were a little spark carried about the body and stowed away in some obscure recess, but it would be more true to say that it is the soul which carries the body about. . . . Man, we are learning, is not a body possessing a soul, but a soul possessing a body. . . . This conviction of the body's worth and its infinite possibilities will surely never wane in Christendom; for every birth is a microcosm of the Incarnation, and every baby born a little word of God made flesh."*

If we should persistently think of the body as the temple of the Holy Spirit, it would always appear to us as it appears in Spirit and in Truth. We should have no occasion to think of it as limited, ailing, or weak. We should know it as God's Temple, whole, perfect, and complete.

BECAUSE MY BODY IS GOD'S TEMPLE OF PER-FECTION, I SEE IT HENCEFORTH AS GOD SEES IT.

THE UNIFYING PROCESS

If one is to get the most out of life, the three elements of his mind must be coordinated to bring health, supply, success, and happiness. Our program starts by getting a clearer understanding of the nature of the work to be done and the tools to be used. The tools, of course, are our ideas and thoughts. The equipment is the conscious mind. The work is to unify and train the mind to think along constructive lines under every circumstance. First, the faculties must be unified around the Master Center, which is Christ; then they must be extended until they become a part of the Superconscious Mind. Finally, they must be turned within until the whole being is fused and awakened in Spiritual consciousness.

The unifying process can be compared to the "magnetizing of the iron bar which sets the attractive power of each molecule within the bar to working with all the rest, instead of in an

* *Quoted from Dr. Dearmer in THE HEALING EVANGEL by Dr. A. J. Gayner Banks.*

opposite direction or at right angles," says Paul Ellsworth; he believes too that "The effectiveness of the individual is increased a thousand fold when this unifying process is even partially accomplished" and bemoans the fact that "in the world of common affairs there is no master motive sufficiently powerful to dominate and coordinate all the others."[*]

Two important functions of the conscious mind are the power of choice and the ability to serve as an inlet to the subconscious. The subconscious mind chooses what shall be done, and the subconscious furnishes the power and form. Let it be understood that nothing ever manifests on the surface (in body or affairs) unless it has previously been accepted and stored in the subconscious. Yes, everything that has ever happened to you was first accepted as an idea in the conscious mind and later passed on to the subconscious. "Oh, but I never thought of the particular disease I had," you say. Nevertheless, the experience could not have manifested for you unless at some time it had been stored beneath the level of consciousness. It could not come in any other way.

We can protect ourselves by unifying our conscious and subconscious minds with the consciousness of the Absolute. Let us tell ourselves many times a day the words that David sang so long ago:

"AS THE HART PANTETH AFTER THE WATER BROOK, SO PANTETH MY SOUL AFTER THEE, OH GOD."

* *Ellsworth, Paul. THE UNIFYING PROCESS.*

THE DIVINE IDEA

"There is a spirit in man; and the inbreathing of the Almighty giveth him understanding." JOB 32:8.

Just as the lungs breathe in the air that purifies, cleanses, and renews the body, the Spirit breathes in the Life and Wisdom of God that give power and understanding to the mind. Since the Mind always develops what we give it (what we habitually believe ourselves to be), it is of the greatest importance that we identify ourselves with the inner (spiritual) man instead of with the outer (material) man and that we affirm the Truth of our being instead of its error.

"But we all, with open face beholding as in a glass the glory of the Lord are changed into the same image from glory to glory, even as by the spirit of the Lord." "If we hold steadfastly before it [the thought] the divine idea and believe in its realization," says Richard Lynch, "it will recreate the body in accordance with its mental pattern. The body is healed only as the thought is healed. It is a true record of ideas and takes its own vengeance upon a miscreator. It must be spiritualized by the perception and recognition of its eternal perfection in Divine Mind. There is but One Mind, and the health of man's body, being in that Mind, can never be impaired or lost. When the concept of this spiritual body is revealed to man, healing becomes the most normal thing in the world. It is impossible for the body to manifest pain or disease if the thought which miscreated it is destroyed."*

"There is a natural man, and there is a spiritual man." There is an outer man, and there is an inner man. There is a man of flesh, and a man "from God, a house not made with hands,

* *Lynch, Richard. USABLE TRUTH.*

eternal in the heavens." Then, how shall we glorify God in our bodies and give the spiritual man absolute sovereignty and power in our lives? By dropping from our minds all the false beliefs and pictures we have held concerning the outer man and by contemplating the Divine Ideal. When we keep the channel to the Infinite clear by recognizing only the Real Man, blessings beyond our power to anticipate come without call. When we block the channel by our unbelief, by our wilful living, by our surrender to the demands of the natural man, the cargo of Good remains unclaimed in the open sea.

CHAPTER 13

RE-EDUCATING THE SUBCONSCIOUS MIND

When the subconscious mind does not function normally (in harmony with good), we may be sure that the thoughts and patters of the conscious mind are responsible. In some way or other, we have given the subconscious mind the wrong image, thought, or belief to work on. We have turned some negative experience or idea over and over in our minds until a disease or a failure-dealing habit has been formed.

In re-educating the subconscious mind, we cut the roots of destructive beliefs by talking ourselves out of them, and plant new and different types of thought seeds by talking ourselves into them. In dealing with subconscious limitations and weaknesses, we are dealing pretty largely with negative and undisciplined habits of thought. By breaking (changing the polarity) of a bad mental habit and by forming a good one, we can get the correct result.

Jesus warned us of the importance of purifying and re-educating the subconscious mind in His references to cleansing the outside of the cup and platter and leaving the inside uncleansed, to removing withered and unfruitful branches, and to uprooting cumbersome plants. Man's life and experience are made up of all that he has thought, felt, and said; consequently, his consciousness contains many beliefs that must be cast out before his life can be wholly good. He must talk himself out of all his errors, fill in his omissions, and initiate new causes. Through re-education, his subconscious mind must be cleared of old unfruitful and negative beliefs, and given new wholesome patters of thought. Everything that is working against the good of man must be expelled from his subconscious mind. Death-dealing beliefs must be destroyed, and new healthful thought structures must be erected.

That is what talking ourselves out of the wrong things can accomplish for us. We are not changing God in this process but changing our relationship to the Law. We are making "straight the way of the Lord" so that our good can get to us automatically. When the ugly and distorted causes have been wiped out, the ugly and distorted effect will be changed.

DIRECTING THE SUBCONSCIOUS

Until the subconscious mind is disciplined, schooled, and directed, it is like a spoiled and unruly child. It will get its owner into all sorts of difficulty, mischief, and trouble. Reasoning deductively and having no volition or power of choice, it will accept the bad as readily as the good. Like the child, it will believe and act upon anything that it receives. Being creative, it will always create in the direction in which it is applied. That is why a perfect model must be kept before it constantly and why it must never be left on its own. Our consciousness must be held to a positive and steadfast affirmation of the good; we must not lose this state of consciousness even for a moment. This steadfastness is what St. Paul meant by "Praying without ceasing."

Just as a child can be trained by sympathetic heart-to-heart talks, by reason and kindness, the subconscious mind can be trained, too. When a child is incorrigible and stubborn, the best discipline is not corporal punishment, denunciation, and scolding, but wise counsel, love, reason, and guidance. So it is with the subconscious mind. By putting things right up to your subconscious self and handling your personal weaknesses, limitations, and mistakes without gloves, you can talk the inner self around any obstacle or over any barrier standing in your way. When you have hauled your subconsciousness over the coals, so to speak, you are ready to direct the power into new channels.

Having negated, through repeated heart-to-heart talks with yourself, the false beliefs of the racial mind and those other beliefs reported to you by the body, you must then get the subconscious mind to accept the new image or pattern you want reproduced. First, you empty your consciousness by dissolving the old patterns (talking yourself out of them); and second, you substitute the perfect model and perpetuate it in your consciousness. The laws of God will do the rest; they will bring forth whatever you may be seeking and will dissolve whatever you do not wish to retain. In a word, you have simply reversed the action of the Law. Instead of being positive to a negative as you once were, you are now positive to a positive. You raze the obstructions, you give the orders — and the subconscious does the work.

LET GO

"Put off the old man and put on the new which is Christ." EPH. 4:22-24; COL. 3:9-10.

Before one can destroy the appearance of disease in the body, he must first destroy the patterns in the mind. The causes of all the undesirable conditions and circumstances in life are in the subconscious mind. A man may spend a lifetime trying to get rid of these false images with the conscious mind and make no headway at all. But when the pattern in the subconscious mind is destroyed, the manifestation too is ended. Consequently, knowing how to change subconscious trends is of supreme importance to the Truth student.

If the subconscious mind governs and controls all the actions and forces of the mind and body and if it is obedient to our word, it will initiate any action which the conscious mind and will may direct. Talking to ourselves about the things we wish to attract or to expel from our experience is really the action of the conscious mind upon the subconscious.

Our chief concern in this lesson is to learn how to let go of undesirable thought patterns in the mind, but let us first see this law at work in some of the ordinary movements of the body. Let us suppose, for instance, that you pick up a potato which you do not know is hot. Before you can pick it up, the conscious mind and will act upon the subconscious; and before you can drop it, the same process has to be repeated. The conscious mind not only has to tell the subconscious that the object is hot but also to tell it to let go of the object. This is a very simple explanation of the process involved in letting go, but it clearly illustrates the principle which must be employed. If all disagreeable conditions are caused, fed, and held in place by subconscious beliefs, then to destroy the beliefs also destroys the effect of the beliefs.

We shall become proficient in this work not by trying to drive the unwanted things out by will or conscious activity, but by quietly and firmly directing the subconscious to let go. Since God has the right-of-way in our consciousness and has made no provision for trouble and disease, we must convince the subconscious that there is no law to support them. When this conviction takes place, evil vanishes into its native nothingness.

RELEASE AND BE RELEASED

The Law of Mind is a two-way law. It will repel evil as well as attract good. It will let go as readily as it will take hold. It will lift a man up as quickly as it will let him down. "To him that hath shall be given." Given what? Given more of what he already hath. The Law does not act upon our desires, hopes, or wishes but upon our mental acceptance. It creates more of what our consciousness is already filled with because there is nothing in us which denies the things we are filled with. The Law will create for us the things we should like to have when there is nothing in us to deny their existence. Disagreeable conditions indicate the kinds of thought we are entertaining. Release the thought, and you change the condition.

Obviously, therefore, we cannot have the things and conditions we want until we have released the things and conditions we do not want. Two things cannot occupy the same space at the same time, any more than two thoughts can occupy the same mind at the same time. The world is full of people today who are trying to pick up things with hands that are already full, who are trying to attract things they cannot hold. St. Luke said, "Release, and ye shall be released." Put down the thought of limitation you are entertaining, you will then be free to pick up the good.

The metaphysical ostrich will tell you not to recognize evil in any form. His advice is to refuse to face the condition by sticking your head in the sand and saying that everything is all right when everything is all wrong, Jesus said, "Agree with thine adversary quickly." Seeing the evil as an effect of the subjective state of your thought and not as a part of yourself is half the battle. The other half is to substitute the constructive thought for the destructive one.

BECAUSE I KNOW THAT THIS CONDITION IS THE RESULT OF THE ACTIVITY OF MY THOUGHT, I COMMAND YOU, MY SUBCONSCIOUS MIND, TO REMOVE THIS THOUGHT FROM MY CONSCIOUSNESS FOREVER. IT DOES NOT BELONG TO ME. IT HAS NO CLAIM ON ME, AND I REFUSE TO HAVE ANYTHING MORE TO DO WITH IT.

TALK YOURSELF OUT OF SICKNESS

Before treating yourself or others, it is advisable to get into a calm, quiet, peaceful, and relaxed state of mind. Subject every thought to the peace, power, love and faith of Jesus Christ, for His peace conditions the mind, transmutes pain, relaxes nerves, muscles, and tendons. His power dissolves friction, strife, and fear. His Love renews, restores, vitalizes, and equalizes all the forces of the body; His Faith effaces worry, doubt, and anxiety, and removes all barriers to your word and its successful operation.

When every thought has been brought into captivity, the next step is to establish connection with the subconscious mind and direct it toward the things you wish carried out. Impress the ideas gently and firmly upon the inner mind until you feel the quickening and renewing that tells you your words have reached the subconscious, that the two minds have become integrated. Quietly and unerringly, the accomplishing word will be involved in your mind. New health and strength will shine out from your whole being. The vitalizing action of God will be quickened in your consciousness, and your body will become alive with His Spirit.

After your conscious mind has grasped the Truth, you must being it forth through the action of the subconscious mind. You must speak to the inner mind as you would speak to another person:

> Subconscious Mind of Me, I am going to put you to a test today that I know you will meet. Take this belief of sickness now operating in my life and cause me to know that it is no part of me. It is not person, place, nor thing; it has no sustaining principle. You know that this is true, and that is why I am directing you to dissolve this belief for me now. You can do it and I know that you will.

When this contact has been established, give your treatment in words like the following:

God's Law of health is the only law operating in my life. Help me to know this truth, to believe it, to accept it, and to make it my own.

JESUS CHRIST IS NOW WITH ME RAISING ME TO HIS CONSCIOUSNESS OF WHOLENESS. Charge my mind with this mighty, freeing, electrifying fact until it penetrates every organ, nerve, atom, and cell.

Help me to behold my body as it is in Spirit—God's perfect temple of wholeness and health. Free my consciousness from all beliefs in disease, weakness, contagion, congestion, mortality, and limitation so that my body may express its perfect and spiritual character.

I know that you have already started work on this commission because I can feel the good effect in my body. I thank you and bless you for your goodness to me. I know that you will continue this work until I am every whit whole.

TALK YOURSELF OUT OF FEAR

Subconscious Mind of Me, I am going to give you a good talking-to. In the past you have had things too much your own way; now there is going to be a change. From here on, you are going to mend your ways and do exactly as I say. You have allowed me to live in a world of uncertainty, bondage, and fear; now you are going to take me into a world of confidence, freedom, and faith. From this day forward, you are going to give up the old beliefs that have been working to my harm, and you are going to entertain only those that work for my good. You are going to give up every belief that contradicts or repudiates the courage, power, and fearlessness I have in Christ. Since I can think only one thought at a time, you are going to fill that thought with a firm, unwavering trust in God as the one and only source of all my good.

I am talking to you, my Subconscious Mind, and I want you to hear, register, and act upon every word and direction I give you. Today, I want you to repudiate every fear, to renounce every belief in evil, and to accept the Good as supreme, true, and absolute. I want you to fill my mind so full of the consciousness of the Presence of God that there is no longer any room in it for the dread, inadequacy, hardship, and perplexity of fear. Help me to know that God is here and that He is working for me every moment of my life. Put everything else out of my mind, every adverse, discordant, and troublesome thought, every dread, doubt, and uncertainty, and every evil belief.

God has not given me "the spirit of fear but of power, and of love, and of a sound mind." Let this word be assimilated by my whole world. Let it uplift and liberate me from every adverse and destructive belief. God in the midst of me is mighty; He will discipline every disobedient thought in my mind, and adjust every discordant condition in my life. God is helping me now. The Lord God Omnipotent reigneth — the Mighty God, the Prince of Peace, with His vitalizing, healing, and transforming power. Send this message over every nerve fibre in my body. Send it to every sanguine cell. Send it to every organ and function. Send it to every gloomy and pessimistic belief and to the darkest corner of my mind. Send it now. Send it hundreds of times every day. Help me to know that wherever I am God is, and that where God is there is nothing to fear. You are doing these things for me now, and I am already feeling the good effects of your work. I thank you.

Robert A. Russell

CHAPTER 14

PURIFYING THE STREAM OF CONSCIOUSNESS

Think of your consciousness as a mirror reflecting the objects which are held before it. Now, can you se that to get a different result in the world of effects, you must hold a different object before the mirror of your consciousness? In metaphysics, this principle is called "The Law of Substitution." It means simply that in order to get rid of one belief, you must substitute another for it, that in order to drop one thought, you must put another in its place. This letting go is easy on the physical plane; all you have to do in order to drop something you are holding is to open your hand. On the mental plane, the process is much more difficult and complicated. You cannot drop things here by a conscious act such as the simple opening of your hand. You cannot get rid of a false belief simply by saying that you no longer hold to it. You can eliminate it only by putting another belief in its place.

The Law of Mind says that you cannot entertain two thoughts at the same time any more than you can walk in opposite directions at the same time. If I tell you not to think of the broken door bell, your mind is immediately directed to it. If you resolve that you are not going to think about the door bell, you are thinking about it. But suppose that neighbor comes in the back door and engages you in conversation that absorbs all your interest and attention. What has happened to your thought about the door bell? You forgot about it, didn't you? When you transferred your thought from the door bell to the neighbor, you were using the Law of Substitution. You substituted one thought for another.

But let us suppose that you have a preponderance of negative thoughts and beliefs to cope with, and let us assume that many of them are very old. An accumulation of old negative beliefs drives one almost to the point of despair; and presumably, you have been fighting this accumulated evil for years. Now you have had a glimpse of Truth and you ask, "Will one constructive idea persistently held clean up the whole sorry mess?" The answer is "Yes." Hold this idea: THE SPIRIT OF CHRIST IN ME NOW PENETRATES AND DISPELS EVERY INHARMONIOUS CONDITION IN MY LIFE. Change your thought into it and keep it changed. Talk to yourself about it day and night, with the conscious mind in the day time and through the subconscious mind at night. Meet every adverse incident with it. Rejoice in every evidence of its truth. You will nullify every negative idea regarding your limited environment, and will walk in "newness of life."

THE SPIRIT DESCENDED INTO THE POOL

The best way to purify a stagnant pool of water is to turn a powerful stream of fresh water into it. The fresh water does not care how long the slime and mud have been there, now how the debris got into the pool in the first place. It is not at all concerned as to where the silt and scum came from, nor who threw the tin cans, bottles, and sticks into it. Its only purpose is to purify and clean up the whole mess.

When a man learns how to apply the principle of mathematics to his problems in computation and measurement, they no longer baffle him. He forgets the difficulties he experienced, and the incorrect results he produced; when he understands the rule, he goes on from there.

If a woman has electricity installed in her house, it is not necessary for her to dwell on the previous inconvenience of being without it. Nor does it make any difference to the efficiency of the electricity why she didn't have its comforts and convenience before. All she has to do now is to press the button, and her house is filled with light.

So it is with a person who has learned how to apply the principle of Truth to his daily problems. It is not necessary for him to remember the mistakes and confusion brought into his life by ignorance (acting in opposition to the principle); he can be content to apply the knowledge of correct principle to solve his present problems.

"And straightway the Spirit descended into the pool and troubled the water" — and God (Good) was revealed. The spirit is the inflowing stream of Truth. The pool is the subconscious mind infested with false beliefs, opinions, gossip, and evil; the descent of spirit is the realization or penetration of the word that will clean out the pool instantly. When the pool is troubled by the mighty inrush of fresh water, the rubbish is brought to the surface and carried off.

THE PARABLE OF THE TARES

We read in the thirteenth chapter of the Gospel according to St. Matthew the story of a farmer who had sown his field with wheat. He had saved the best seed for the new sowing, but an enemy came while he slept and sowed darnel among the wheat. Now darnel looks very much like wheat but is poisonous to eat. While the wheat was in the blade, the deception was not clear, and the farmer did not know that his crop had been fouled. "But when the blade sprang up and brought forth fruit, there appeared the tares also. And the servants of the householder came and said unto him, Sir, didst thou not sow good seed in thy field? From whence then hath it tares? And he said unto them, an enemy hath done this. The servants said unto him, Wilt thou then that we go and gather them up? But he said, Nay; lest while ye gather up the tares, ye root up the wheat with them. Let both grow together until the harvest; and in time of harvest I will say to the reapers, Gather ye together first the tares, and bind them in bundles to burn them: but gather the wheat into my barn."

There is a lesson in this parable that no Truth student should miss. Symbolically, the field is the soul or subconscious mind. It, too, is a bewildering mixture of good and evil—of wheat and tares. Just as the tares warred against the good harvest, negative thinking, lack of vigilance, or the wrong use of the law wars against our spiritual welfare. What is to be done? Two methods are suggested in the parable. The servants were all for the frontal attack. When weeds appeared, they wanted to center attention upon them and pull them up, regardless of what might happen to the wheat growing beside them. Theirs is the negative method. If we follow their advice we shall, when disease appears, treat the disease. If an enemy is present, we shall attempt to destroy him by a direct attack. But the farmer's method was different. He destroyed the tares by a stronger growth of wheat; he let them both grow until they could be separated easily at harvest time. If we apply the Master's method to our thinking and practice, we shall center our attention upon the good and forget the evil, knowing that good and evil are but manifestations of the same power. We shall heal the sick man by building health. We shall destroy evil by cultivating a greater consciousness of the good. We will be positive to Good.

THE EMPTY HOUSE

In *The Parable of the Empty House*, told in the eleventh chapter of the Gospel according to St. Luke, Jesus teaches a lesson that you can readily prove for yourself by a familiar physical experiment. Simply take a bell jar with an outlet and place it over a vessel full of water. Then pump the air out, and the water will rush in. It is Nature's habit to fill a space that has been emptied. This house of which Jesus speaks is empty; and like neutrality, emptiness can be dangerous. To drive out evil thoughts, beliefs, and other impurities and leave the house of the mind unoccupied can be disastrous. Jesus issues a warning which is the inner meaning of the story.

In Jesus' day, people believed that all human ills, deficiencies, and calamities were the result of demoniac possession and obsession. A man's worst enemies were conceived as those in the invisible. His greatest fears were of the unseen malignities floating in the air and waiting to pounce upon him. Science has long since disproved these theories, but medical science is beginning to see that there is a definite connection between the disease patterns of the mind and the diseased conditions of the body. Jesus met these demon-ridden minds and potentates of darkness with the Word of God. He healed the sick, exorcised devils, and cast out demons; and then He gave the same freeing power to us. "Behold, I cast out demons and I do cures." The church is awakening once more to its responsibility for the health of the body as well as for the health of the soul; it is learning that body and soul are two ends of the same thing and that many of those that are sick in the body are first sick in the soul.

But Jesus is concerned in this story with a man who had cast out all evil thoughts and tendencies from his mind and soul and had nothing better to put in their place. He had failed to fill the vacuum (created by the departure of evil) with the Presence of God. So, as Jesus said, "The last state of that man was worse than the first." The lesson is clear: If the expulsion of evil is to be permanent, we must put something bigger, better, and stronger in the place of evil. For wrong activity, we must substitute right activity. When we banish evil, we must welcome Christ. When we really cure disease, we establish and maintain health.

CHAPTER 15

THE PARABLE OF THE TALENTS

In the teachings of Jesus, the Kingdom of God is the Kingdom of Reality, Wholeness, Goodness, Abundance, Order, and Perfection—a Kingdom that is accessible to every man while he is still upon the earth. That is why Jesus prayed, "Thy Kingdom come: Thy will be done in earth as it is in Heaven." Metaphysically interpreted, the Kingdom of God and the Will of God are in essence the very same thing. The Kingdom of God has nothing to do with the outer world, It is first a recognition, next a realization, and then a revelation. The person whose thinking, conversation, and living are in harmony with it will never lack anything; his needs will always be supplied.

In *The Parable of the Talents*, as told in Chapter 25 of the Gospel according to St. Matthew, Jesus likened the Kingdom of God to a man who is about to leave on a long journey and who calls his servants together to deliver his goods to them. "To one he gives five talents, to another two, and to another one." The parable is a lesson on the use and neglect of spiritual endowments. It is the answer to the prevailing belief in the inequality of supply. If one wishes to lose his endowments (the energies and powers which God has given him), he lets them alone. If he wishes to multiply them, he puts them to work.

The parable has three parts: (1) The presentation of the gifts, (2) The use that was made of them, (3) The according, or reckoning.

Let us look first at the presentation. Every man was given something to go on. We all differ in opportunities for increasing our endowments, but we all share the same Mind. We all have the same potentialities. It is not our endowments that determine the increase, but the use we make of them. "Every man begins," said Henry Ford, "with all there is." The essence and substance of all there is is here with us now, and we can appropriate and use it.

The three differed greatly in their use of the talents. The five-talent man was a shrewd investor. He had a consciousness of supply and doubled his investment. The two-talent man doubled his gift also, but he did it through sheer force and physical effort. The third man was a different type. He was both afraid and slothful. He buried his gift in the earth; that is, he neglected it. He neither sensed the responsibility that it imposed nor the possibility of its increase. With every gift, there is a corresponding responsibility. If the gift is neglected, it atrophies; if it is used, it increases in size and power.

The third part of the parable is the reckoning. The central figure in the drama, of course, is the one-talent man. Two of the men were commended for their faithfulness, but the third man lost his gift. "Take ye away, therefore, the talent from him, and give it unto him that hath ten talents, For unto everyone that hath shall be given, and he shall have abundance: but from him that hath not shall be taken away even that which he hath." The increase in the parable went to the man who was already the richest. The increase today goes to him who is already rich in consciousness.

THE INNER MEANING OF THE PARABLE

If there is one thing in the Bible that might stir up resentment, it is the verse in *The Parable of the Talents* that says: "For unto him that hath shall be given, and he shall have abundance: but from him that hath not shall be taken away even that which he hath." "It is cruel! It is unjust!" you say wrathfully. "It is a gross violation of human rights. It might be all right for the rich to give to the poor, but to take from the poor to give to the rich is a disgraceful and intolerable procedure."

But wait a minute. You are reading into the story something which is not there. Jesus was not talking about material possessions but about the law of supply and demand. He is making an out-and-out statement of Divine Law. He is saying that the faithful use of what we have will bring us rich rewards. He is also giving us the steps which we must take in developing a consciousness of abundance. We do not get excited and resentful when we are told that three times three makes nine instead of ten. We do not get mad when we are told that "Like attracts like," or that "Matter expands when heated," that "Water seeks its own level," or that "Whatsoever a man soweth, that shall he also reap." We are delighted to know that the universe in which we live is dependable and law abiding. Then why should we resent this specific law?

When we understand the law, we shall see that it is the means of building a mighty measure of the Kingdom of God within ourselves. Jesus was not talking about external circumstances or concrete possessions but about mental states, or degrees of consciousness. One man had a cumulative consciousness (had the good in abundant measure). One had a divided consciousness (had the good in limited measure). The other man had an inert or letting-go consciousness (had nothing in the end).

Let us remember that the basis of all attraction or loss is in the consciousness of man and not in outer circumstances or conditions or things. It makes no difference what a man may be seeking, whether it be mental, material, or spiritual riches. If his consciousness is cumulative in a given direction, he will positively accumulate in that direction. Rich men are not determined by favorable opportunities or circumstances, nor poor men by the lack of them. Their richness and poorness depend upon the construction, tendency, and use of their minds. "To him that hath shall be given and from him that hath not, even that which he hath shall be taken away." This law holds good on every plane of life; it means simply that the increase of possession is the result of a cumulative consciousness and their loss is the result of an inert or indifferent consciousness. Since each individual determines his own type of consciousness, talking one's self out of the indifferent and into the cumulative consciousness becomes an immediate obligation.

MAKING AN APPRAISAL

Most of us are with our talents like the man who buried his gift in the earth. We have latent powers, locked-up abilities, undiscovered possibilities, enormous reserves, countless resources, immortal capital upon which we never draw. We are beggars sitting on bags of gold. Out talents are legion, but they are lying idle. We never do anything to stir them up and to bring them out. Jesus was very hard on the one-talent man, you recall. He had the same possibilities as the other two men, but he failed to develop them. He had no interest to show because he had made no investment.

We feel sorry for the one-talent man, not because of his fear and sloth but because of his wasted possibilities and lost opportunity. The emphasis of the parable is not upon God's investment but upon man's return. For every gift, God demands an accounting of us. For every planting, He demands a harvest. The law is inexorable. We must use or lose. If we handle our gifts poorly, they are lessened or withdrawn.

Let me consider what talents I have neglected. What are they? First, God has given me a mind and the power to think. I can choose my aspirations, attitudes, beliefs, convictions, feeling, and thoughts. I can create and mold my own destiny. At the center of my being, I have access to all power; but if I use only a small measure of power, I am carrying part of it hidden. If I use it to create evil instead of good, I am perverting it and impoverishing myself.

I also have a talent for authority, dominion, patience, thanksgiving, and forgiveness; a talent for cooperation, industry, diligence, and dispatch; a talent for joy, faith, renewal, blessing, courage, health, strength, prosperity, confidence, peace, tolerance, service, enthusiasm, and kindness.

I have the power to see what I want to see and to do what I want to do. I have the power to rise or fall, to be strong or weak, rich or poor. If I am not actively using these talents, I am burying them in the ground. If I say, "I am afraid," "I can't," "I am worn out," or "I am sick," I too am judged and condemned for my non-use of the talent for life.

Robert A. Russell

CHAPTER 16

MIND AND NOT-MIND

I do not have a mind. I am Mind. I am the Mind of God unrealized. I am the Universal Mind in miniature. I am the microcosm in the Macrocosm. I live, move, and have my being in Mind, and I shall never leave it. I am in the midst of a Creative mind that acts upon the thoughts I impress upon it. I am in this Mind, and this Mind is in Me. It is the power by which I think. It is to me what I am to It. It responds to me by corresponding to my states of thought. It is God's Mind and my mind at the same time. My mind is not another mind but God's Mind manifesting as me. The Highest Mind and the innermost mind are one mind. I am the Divine Mind in essence and the human mind in manifestation. I am the Mind of God on a small scale and the mind of myself on a large scale. I am the Mind of Christ in the seed and the mind of mortality in the blade. I am Mind and Its thinking. Everything in my home, business, and environment is what I think it is. It can never be anything else, for persons, places, conditions, and things have no existence apart from my mind. I am my mind; therefore, everything must be to me what I think it is. Everything that I am is what it is because of what I think I am. It is both the good and the evil because there is nothing good nor bad but thinking makes it so.

I am also a not-mind. It is the absolute antithesis of what I am in essence. I know my Real Mind only by what I have failed to accomplish through this not-mind. My failures and mistakes are but the manifestations of my non-use of the

Real Mind. This not-mind was created not by God but by me. It is the cause of all my sin, trouble, sickness, and distress. When I try to know the Truth in this mind, I fail, for it is incapable of knowing the truth. How, then, can I displace it? By talking it out of myself and by letting my Real Mind take possession. What will happen then? I shall find that I have absolute dominion over every circumstance and condition in my life. I shall have the solution to every problem, the cure for every disease, the fulfillment of every need, the correction for every mistake, the salvation for every sin, the adjustment for every difficulty, the truth for every error, and the answer to every prayer.

THINKING WITH THE MIND OF CHRIST

Unless one thinks with the Mind of Christ, he is not really thinking at all. He is merely a sounding board for the thoughts of others. Thinking without a source (by reflection), he is like a phonograph recording only what others say. He is like a man breathing his own air. He is thinking in a circle, an action like that of a dog chasing its tail. We are told to repent and change our mind. Change it from what to what? From the carnal to the spiritual, from self to Christ. Thinking with the human mind is like the action of a man trying to lift himself by his own bootstraps. Both are without power and without results. That is why St. Paul said: "Let this Mind be in you which was also in Christ Jesus." What is this Mind which was also in Christ Jesus? It is our Savior. It is the Mind of Abraham, Isaac, and Jacob. It is our mind, too. Then how are we to have no other mind but His? By thinking in one direction—toward Good without doubt or compromise. It is the difference between thinking from the Source of Life or from the circumference. It is the difference between Immaculate Perception and human fumbling.

As Jesus pointed out, thinking with God is thinking by indirection, or without effort. "Take no thought for your life, what ye shall eat or what ye shall drink." Take no thought for your body. Take no thought for the future. "Your Heavenly Father knoweth that ye have need of all these things;" and when you have no other Mind but His, they will be supplied without any intervention of the carnal mind whatsoever.

At the center of man's being, he is essentially whole and perfect. At the circumference, he is confused and divided by his adulterated thinking. To put it plainly, he is thinking in the human mind, ignoring the Mind of Christ. It is not a sin of commission but of omission. What is the remedy? To begin thinking *in* and *with* the Mind of Christ. How does one do that? By refusing to entertain human thoughts, beliefs, or opinions; by refusing to accept the testimony of the sense; and by seeing God as everywhere evenly present.

THE SPIRITUAL LAW OF ADJUSTMENT

When we recognize that all the Power in the Universe is on the side of Good, that the Law of Good has the power to enforce itself, and that there is no law to support what is not good, we shall have a means of adjusting and harmonizing every discordant condition in our lives. St. Paul said, "The law of the Spirit of life in Christ Jesus hath made me free from the law of sin and death." The "law of sin and death" (negative creation and experience) has nothing to back it up—nothing to support it. It is a parasite. It operates only on borrowed power (through a divided and adulterated consciousness); it is, therefore, temporary and unreal.

We can use this Law of Cause and Effect in any way we choose, but It will always be to us what we are to It. If we have been using It to create bondage, we can now use It to create freedom. We do not use two powers, however, but use one Power in two ways. Like the law which causes iron to sink in one form and to float in another form, the law that has caused disease and failure can produce both health and success. The change by which this metamorphosis is brought about is not in the law but in our mental position, or relation to it.

"The law of the Spirit of Life" is self-operative. We have absolutely no responsibility for its execution. The only thing we can do in solving a problem of any kind is to involve the law (declare the Truth) and then put the problem out of our thought. When we have done this (recognized the law as present and in operation), we have brought the whole Presence and Power of God to bear upon our problem, and whatever is unlike God will be cast away.

But how, you ask, can a law that is purely spiritual change a condition that is purely physical? The answer is clear when you understand that the problem itself is mental and not physical. There cannot be a problem without a mind to create and sustain it. That is why you are told to resolve the problem theoretically into mind and then change your thought about it. When you have done this, you have done everything that can be done. You have brought the Law of Spirit into contact with your problem. Where the Spirit is, there is freedom, harmony, and order.

SETTING THE LAW IN MOTION

Before we set the spiritual law in motion, let us first consider the conditions necessary to its operation. There are three:

1. The recognition that the only adjustment that has to be made is in the human mind.

2. The desire of the human mind to surrender its preconceived opinions, beliefs, attitudes and feelings.

3. The willingness to let God have full responsibility for harmonizing every discordant condition.

It makes no difference where we find ourselves today — in the vicious circle of slander, the vacuum of misdeeds, the slough of doubt, the swamp of failure, the maze of habit, or the quagmire of disease. It makes no difference what the problem or trouble may be. The moment we appeal to the Spiritual Law of Adjustment and fulfill the conditions of its operation, the moment we relinquish our beliefs and recognize that the Law is now at work in the problem or need, it will take possession of our minds and harmonize, heal, and correct whatever is out of adjustment with the Divine Will. It is not the action of the human will that brings order out of chaos and good out of evil, however, but our willingness to let God dominate every situation through the operation of His own Law.

In the human consciousness, our present problem may seem beset with impossible odds. In the Christ consciousness, everything is already in its right place. The evil that appears is what the human mind believes. How can we remove the cause of evil/ By reversing our beliefs and by using the Law in a better way. Instead of using the Law to create the undesirable, we can use it to create the desirable. The Law, which is always in operation, does not take from the rich man and give to the poor, nor does it withhold from some and give to others. It serves all alike.

Then what shall we do when we find ourselves embroiled in argument, or victims of unjust criticism? The first thing is to impersonalize the incident. We must give it no power from us that we do not have to take it into our hands. If the Spiritual Law of Adjustment equalizes, harmonizes, governs, and regulates all discordant conditions, our part is to assume no responsibility beyond realizing that the Law of God is at work bringing a correct and satisfactory solution to the problem. No matter how grave or serious the problem may be, the answer will come if we stop the conscious thinking (get ourselves out of the way).

RATIONALIZING THE IDEA OF DEATH

The best way to treat the idea of death is to practice a happy indifference toward it. If there is only One Life — the Life of God which is in us and in which we are, and if there is only one existence, it is quite obvious that the life we are now living is the only life we shall ever have. Made in the Image of Likeness of God, man is birthless, deathless, and imperishable. What we call death is simply a waking up to the knowledge that we have not died. It is a revelation of the self to the self. Being immortal already, we did not have to become immortal. Being full-orbed, we did not have to grow. Being in the Kingdom of God and having the Kingdom of God in us, we did not have to go somewhere else. We simply stayed where we were and became conscious of more than we had previously known. "Now I know in part, but then I shall know even as also I am known." Our life in the flesh is half sleep and half waking. Out life in the Spirit will be all waking.

We must not think of death as an enemy but as a friend helping us into our new and larger life. Just as birth was a door into this life, death will be a door into renewed life. It is like Christmas and Easter. Christmas is a birth into the seen; Easter is a birth into the unseen. They are two ends of the same thing — life and renewed life. What we have mistakenly called the afterlife, or the future life, is simply a continuation of this life without he impediments of a fleshly mind and material law. As St. Paul tells us in his First Epistle to the Corinthians, we shall find the soul after death clothed in a wholly spiritual body of its own making.

It is our duty to live out our span, but let us not shudder when the summons come. The whole problem is solved when we realize the eternalness of our own being. "Before Abraham was I am." Death loses its sting and the grave its victory when we realize that life did not stop when we leave it. St. Paul said, "For me to die is gain." Then what difference can it make when or how we go? Everyone travels the same road sooner or later because nature will not allow us to congeal. If God is Omnipresent, He is where we are and we are where He is, and there is no coming or going. There is no separation in Spirit.

Robert A. Russell

ACKNOWLEDGEMENTS

The author wishes to make grateful acknowledgement for suggestions and quotations used in this book to the following individuals:

Frederick W. Bailes

Dr. Titus Bull

Dr. A. J. Gayner Banks

Dr. Dearmer

Paul Ellsworth

Charles Fillmore

Dr. J. M. Finnery

Williston M. Ford

Elbert B. Holmes

Ernest Holmes

E. L. House

Richard Lynch

J. L. McIntyre

Dr. W. L. Sadler

Orlando Wanvig

and to

The Forward Movement

and

Sharing

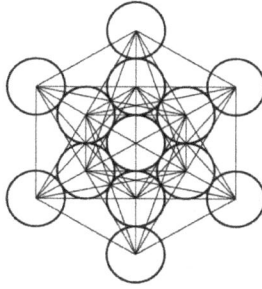

Raisa - Mystic Alchemist

Energy Healing, Chakra Alignment, Sacred Geometry, Sound Healing

Tammy:

I was blessed with a healing session by Raisa last week. She felt like a friend and like-minded gentle soul with comforting Mother Mary essence pouring through her words. Raisa was so in-tuned to my blocks and traumas held within my field. She used her connection to ascended masters I've resonated with such as Yeshua, Mother Mary, Mary Magdalene, Lady Vesta & Amethyst and archangels Metatron, Michael and others to help clear these.

I was able to address childhood trauma situations to flip the stuck energy I've held onto over the years. She also picked up on a few traumatic past-life scenes that have affected my current life. I am an intuitive energy healer who truly felt the shift and healing within. I now feel so much lighter and have clarity regarding my path.

So much love and gratitude to you both, Raisa and Barry for presenting her to my world! (More Testimonials on following Pages)

Contact Raisa to book an Energy Healing
or Chakra Alignment session:
www.RaisinYourIsness.com
raisinyourisness@hotmail.com

Shannon:

This BEAUTIFUL sister...our Raisa... is a treasure beyond compare! After my experience in my personal session with Raisa... the ABSOLUTE confirmation I received, that could ONLY be confirmed by HER mind you... this session solidified EVERYTHING for me. I KNOW that this sister... she is a formidable, magnificent & IRREPLACEABLE component in this Earth plane story we all are invested in! IF YOU ARE DRAWN TO HER FOLLOW YOUR HEART

No other can do what SHE is gifted to do for YOU... YES YOU!

I LOVE YOU dear sister! I am forever grateful for what only you could do and DID for me! I would have happily paid any price for what you gave me! I URGE YOU ALL to schedule a session with this beloved one!

P.S. thank you Barry for sharing her with us all!

∞

Natasha:

I would like to thank Barry for introducing us to Raisa. I have had 2 consultations with her in the last month and I am in total awe of what transpired. Raisa is such a beautiful caring soul! She connected with me as though she has known me forever. Her love and dedication in assisting others is so touching. I had an amazing experience and some profound healing. I received a message from Jeshua which brought tears to my eyes. I could feel the LOVE in the message that was given to me and I will remember and cherish His message forever. Raisa has really helped me in confronting fears, trauma and past life karma. I have found the reason for my skin problems which I never would have thought it'd be possible. It is amazing what guilt and shame from past lives can actually do to your body. Her healing and that from our Angelic beings has really made a huge difference in my life. I can feel it in my energy. Raisa has a lovely sense of humour, always reminding you not to take life and yourself so seriously. I really feel like a heavy weight has been lifted off my soul. Thank you so much! Much Love!

∞

Ariel:

Raisa... Divine Raisa... You are a Treasure to this Life, and I thank All That Is, and this also Treasured YT channel for the priceless blessing which was our session this AM. Every moment of the session was a fractal explosion of wonderful intuitive & divinely guided perfection. I honor your sincere, caring, graceful, playful, soothing, encouraging, transformational, empowering, and so beautiful demonstration / embodiment of Goddess energy and presence. I am so honored & thankful to have been guided to You. To have invested in the patience, time, energy, and resources to share sacred healing and uplifting time with You. I will remember the session Always. And I will look forward to any and all ways our Creator deems it harmonious to connect again. I could go on and on and on, so please accept my parting acknowledgment of your blessing to this realm, my Heart & Spirt, my Life, and the Lives of all those who may be positively impacted via your assistance. Blessings, and Gratitude, a thousand times over and over again. Namaste... Namaste... Namaste...

∞

B.G.

I have just finished a healing session with Raisa. The experience was remarkable! I am still buzzing! I heard about her from this channel, so thank you deeply Barry!

Raisa is so lovely to talk to, and intuitively guided, knows how to get to the hidden roots of our issues. She calls upon ascended masters, archangels and such to do deep energetic clearing and healing work. It was like being guided through the deep layers of myself, releasing the things that don't serve me and filling every cell with light. I purged, and I absorbed new energy, and came out feeling uplifted and renewed. Raisa helped me to find things in myself that I had been cut off from, and to heal wounds I had tried to bury. She has also given me helpful ideas to continue to improve things my life.

I am so blessed to have found Raisa, and ever grateful for the healing work she has done. She is as authentic as they come. Truly an earth angel! Thank you, thank you, thank you!

YouTube

www.ingramcontent.com/pod-product-compliance
Lightning Source LLC
Chambersburg PA
CBHW021338090426
42742CB00008B/648